Ironmind

Ironmind

AGAINST ALL ODDS

Conor Devine

ISBN-13: 9781539877844
ISBN-10: 1539877841

Contents

Chapter 9

Mum and Dad, thank you for all of your love and support over the years, without which I wouldn't be where I am today.

Acknowledgements

would like to take this opportunity to thank the people who have helped me achieve the success I've had in my life, and who have given me the tools and belief to go on to be a better version of myself.

Firstly, anyone considering any kind of endurance challenge will recognise that you have to take a lot of time out of your already-busy schedule to train. It's quite simple, if you don't put in the training and effort required, it's likely you won't realise your goal. I knew from the outset in December 2014, when I devised this challenge, that I needed a certain level of support to complete the training program and challenge I had set myself.

I want to say thank you very much to my mother and father who continue to be my rocks in times of adversity. You've both been extremely encouraging from the get-go, and I wouldn't have been able to complete it without your love, care and support, in particular in looking after my two diamonds, Lilyanna and Conor Junior.

To my sister Ciara and to Jonny, who have always been supportive, thank you for being there when I needed help. To my brother Colm and to Lisa, to whom, again, nothing was ever a problem, and who helped me a lot in preparation for this challenge and throughout the Ironman race in Majorca. Colm, your encouragement – roaring and swearing – when I arrived at transition two, after seven hours and fifty minutes on the bike, completely exhausted, will stay with me for a long time.

I would also like to thank the person who marked my eleven-plus examination in 1988. I failed this exam, and it was the first time in my life I'd experienced a significant disappointment. Thankfully I applied myself, and through sport, initially, gained entry to my first-choice school and ultimately went on to excel academically. It was that failure which primarily made me revisit my own academic position at the time and work out that I needed to apply myself better if I was to attain my academic goals.

Thanks also to the senior scout at Coventry City Football Club. While Coventry were playing in the English Premier League in 1994, their scout thought I was too small and took away my lifelong dream of becoming a professional footballer. This was another major setback for me to overcome; however, despite taking it badly for quite some time, it allowed me to yet again experience adversity, feel and deal with the pain and ultimately go on and grow through that difficult, emotional episode.

In a funny way I'm also grateful for my MS diagnosis as it changed the entire trajectory of my life. Before I got sick I hadn't a care in the world, and, on reflection, like a lot of people, I may have got carried away with the less important things in life. It was through this illness and those very dark days that became months and extended to years that I thankfully discovered the real me and worked out what life was really about.

Someone told me once that it's only through real adversity that one truly grows. I have absolutely no doubt that my diagnosis and illness, once I got my head around it and gained the skill set and determination I needed to get me through it, was the time in my life when I arrived at my crossroads. I had a choice to either go left – give up – or go right – dig deep and achieve my goals and aspirations. Thankfully I chose the right path.

There's no way I could have written this book without the inspiration and strength of my two children. Lilyanna and Conor, one day, when you're a little older, you might both sit back and understand this better, but when

I was ninety miles into my bike ride in Majorca in the sizzling midday sun and wanted to stop, get off the bike and cry as I was in so much pain, it was the thought of seeing you both as I crossed the finishing line that gave me the determination and desire to keep going. Thank you, Lilyanna and Conor. I love you both very much.

There are many others who over the years have helped me, supported me, encouraged me and been there for me in the really hard times and the good times as well – too many to mention, but you all know who you are. Thank you for all the support and encouragement. It's one of the reasons I developed this iron mindset, the one my mum always believed that young boy from Lomond Heights, Cookstown, County Tyrone, would go on to do.

Foreword

Conor Devine is a man on a mission, a mission to live his life every day no matter what is thrown at him.

I've completed a few endurance adventures in my time and helped others who suffer from multiple sclerosis (MS) to complete their own endurance feats; these are two things Conor knows about. Many of us would never associate those who have MS with climbing mountains, running marathons or completing Ironman triathlons, but through the experiences I've had while training MS sufferers, and becoming friends with Conor, I've realised that the disease can be managed and phenomenal physical achievements conquered as long as a positive, never-give-up mindset is present.

I first read about Conor when I stumbled across his inspiring blog. I didn't stop at reading just one of his inspirational pieces of writing, I continued reading the entire content of his website, and I forwarded it to a client of mine a few years ago as they had common interests: MS and a passion for pushing themselves to their limits. Amazed by Conor's journey of overcoming a life-changing setback and then continuing to strive to evolve as a person and make a positive impact in the world, I immediately felt compelled to get in touch with him.

The thing that drew me closer to Conor (apart from a guy who sees no boundaries) is that he questions what the world deems 'normal' and then searches for what the true reality is – not just in relation to what society may think is a normal amount of physical activity for a guy who is living with MS, but also in pretty much everything else he does in life!

As you will read throughout this book, Conor doesn't waste time, energy or effort on the negative things that have happened in his life and which have tried to stop him progressing. Instead, he uses his confident mindset to work with what he has, while continually finding ways to improve himself as a human being. The impact he has had on not only those people around him but also those who have met him or read his story is truly remarkable. The guy has an infectious enthusiasm for life and one of the most positive attitudes I've ever been around. Although Conor initially battled with his diagnosis of MS, he now embraces the fact that he has this autoimmune disease which affects his central nervous system, and he creates awareness, education and, more importantly, hope for many other sufferers of the disease.

I remember Conor telling me about the six-events-in-twenty-weeks idea he was thinking about completing. My initial reaction was excitement for him, and although I knew it was going to be tough, both mentally and physically, I could see the fire in his eyes and knew he would do whatever it took to overcome any hurdles that may get in his way – he had a bellyful of passion to succeed and was ready to do the necessary work! With his increased training for the marathons and triathlons he was preparing to complete during this project, we started sharing many messages about food, nutrition and what the majority of people competing in endurance events actually need to eat before, during and after their training and events. When I told him I only ever eat real food, not processed junk that's branded as 'sports nutrition', it reassured his intelligent and thought-provoking mind that he was correct in his thinking all along: that there is a better way to fuel a body during regular training and racing.

As you will read, Conor is quite passionate about the food he puts in his body, not only during his training and racing but also in everyday life.

Alongside sharing his nutrition, preparation and the ways he mentally prepared for his endurance challenge, Conor takes us on a journey through the six events he chose to complete, starting with Belfast City Marathon. Endurance sports are never straightforward or easy, especially when you're relying on a body with MS to get you through hours and hours of grueling physical strain only for it to recover and within weeks be put through further torment. This is exactly what Conor went through during the twenty weeks he gave himself to complete his goal. Continually pushing his own limits and evolving, not only as an athlete but also as a person, was achieved through creating a clear understanding of what he wanted to accomplish all the while being fuelled by his formula of goal-setting, self-belief, hard work, dedication and loving his own life.

I thoroughly enjoyed Conor's journey as he set out to accomplish what started as a thought, turned into a vision and became a reality. He embraced the setbacks that came his way from both his body and external forces, while maintaining a robust positive attitude to get through many arduous situations that were thrust upon him. What Conor has constantly demonstrated is that what we perceive are our limits are actually the beginning of what we are truly capable of. His journey into the world of inspiring others to dream big and live their lives has just begun.

Thanks, Conor, for taking the time to share this story. You truly do have an Ironmind.

Luke Tyburski
Endurance Adventurer

Introduction

The mind is the athlete the body is just the means

UNKNOWN

Finally I could see the top of the mountain. I'd been climbing for nearly two hours, I was seventy miles into the bike ride, my legs were screaming with pain and my mind was weak. To see the top of the mountain was equivalent to seeing a ten-gallon drum of water in the desert. I knew after this I had approximately ninety minutes of cycling ahead – mostly downhill, thank God for that. I could then start the marathon and would be home and hosed; running was my strongest leg of the event. I was nearly there and a sensational feeling came over my body. I suddenly noticed lots of fellow athletes had dismounted. I stopped to see what was going on and an official with a race supervisor T-shirt came over and told me quite aggressively that my race was over and I was disqualified. For the next sixty seconds I went into deep shock. I was just under six hours into my 112-mile cycle, almost nine hours into my Ironman, what the hell was this tube talking about? I knew I was on time and I would make the seventeen-hour cut-off to complete the Ironman. Who the hell was this guy and what was going on? I ferociously challenged him on his claims. How could this be?

'You are out of the race. It's finished. Goodbye,' he said.

2015 had been an amazing year for me in many ways. Lots of laughs, a great deal of adversity, an abundance of challenges, many tears shed on my own, numerous low points and as many high points, but the Ironman in September was a defining moment in my life.

I wrote my first book in 2012, *Attitude Is Everything*, and published it in 2013 because after speaking to others, I recognised that my story of recovery was powerful, and I felt very strongly that I had to share my journey with the world; of how I was able to fight back and recover from multiple sclerosis. There was a message in that book, and thankfully it has been well received, and even more empowering for me, I know that it went on to help others deal with their own challenges in life. *Ironmind – Against All Odds* has come about for similar reasons. In 2007, when diagnosed with multiple sclerosis, my world fell apart. I couldn't see how to live my life and reach my potential. I had lost all hope and asked myself on many occasions if I could live with my debilitating symptoms while being a drain on everyone around me; it was a really dark, desperate and sad time in my life. I'm hoping, at the very least, that through this book you will see very clearly that with the right plan, a definite sense of purpose and the correct action, absolutely everything is possible. I'm thirty-eight years old, living very well with multiple sclerosis, and over the last ten years I've come to learn the secret of making progress in life. I'll share that secret with you in this book.

This year has been a blessing in that I have added to my mastermind group and continued to grow in all areas. I'm pushing my body and my mind like never before and the journey has been sensational. *Ironmind* is my gift to you. It's my glory lap and an opportunity for me to set out exactly how I took my body and mind from a very dark place through to accomplishing one of the world's most dangerous and testing endurance races. I'm a young man determined to leave my mark on as many people as I can, help them believe in themselves and in doing that assist them in working out how they too can fight and defeat adversity and live an extremely fulfilling life.

I feel truly blessed and grateful that I have this incredible opportunity to let you into my life again to share with you a mindset that can get you from the hospital bed to the lofty position of Ironman. Surely a guy living with multiple sclerosis shouldn't be running his own business, competing in marathons and even considering Ironman endurance races? If you'd spoken to me between 2007 and 2010, I may have agreed with you, but in the last twelve months I've taken my mind and body to places I didn't think existed. It's called the extra mile, and the truth is there aren't many people on that track. It can be one lonely old road, but listen carefully to me: if you want what others have, you have to do what others are not prepared to do.

Ironmind, Against all odds has been an incredible experience. In this journey I've surprised my friends, my family and even myself. The young boy who wanted to play for Manchester United and lived with failure after failure after failure but kept going and wouldn't give up is now an Ironman. I'm really proud of what I've achieved, and you know what the best part is? You too can achieve what you want out of life. All you have to do is develop an iron mind.

I hope you enjoy my book.

CD

CHAPTER 1

Never, never, never give up,
WINSTON CHURCHILL

Christmas Holidays

It had been another busy year at my consultancy practice, GDP Partnership, in Belfast, and I was happy at how my career was progressing. It wasn't always like this, though. Just four years earlier I was frustrated at the direction my career was going. As a young boy playing football for my home town, I promised myself I would do well in life. I've always been interested in business and what makes successful people tick, and, true enough, my career has always been business oriented. I qualified as a chartered surveyor in 2005 and spent eight years cutting my teeth in the property market in Ireland. My interest there developed in my teens and I learned quickly on the job. The industry has been very good to me, especially throughout the legendary Celtic tiger. However, my time with the company I had held a directorship with had ran its course; I had stopped growing professionally and was in my comfort zone. I knew I had to take action if I wanted to change my fortunes and maintain my passion, so I decided, with my new business partner, James, to set up an advisory business and go out on my own. At that time we felt there was a real demand for professional people who had expertise in banking, law and real estate to assist people who had found themselves drowning with property debt, and so the GDP Partnership was born. Nearly five years later, our debt advisory business is now the market leader in the country and the future looks extremely promising.

Hard work is not new to me, and I do put a good shift in all year round, but I have found over the years, as I've got a little bit older and maybe a bit wiser, that Christmas time has become even more precious. It gives me an opportunity to pull the plug out of the wall, step back from the business and immerse myself in family life, which I love. It's also become a hugely important time for me to set out my goals for the year ahead. The drill is, I pick a day between Christmas and the new year, get a few hours on my own away from humans – children and adults, phones, chocolate, Guinness and television, with paper and pen and only my thoughts for company. I review the past year, think about what I could have done better, where I fell short, what I really want in the next twelve months and how I can make it happen. It's simply a time for me to put a plan together of how I propose to become a stronger, better person and version of me. It's really an annual review, a time when I lift the bonnet and ask myself some deep, gut-wrenching questions. It's a chance for me to be completely frank and honest with myself. After a period of quiet (some liken this to meditation) and self-reflection, I write down my goals for the year ahead. The interesting thing about this exercise is that over the last few years I've been able to hit a lot of these goals, which means that I've continued to grow and achieve, the desired outcome.

I was introduced to the concept of personal development in 2010 through a good friend who introduced me to the teachings of Jim Rohn, the American motivational speaker. Jim talked at length about the power of physically writing your goals down on paper as opposed to just thinking about them. Through my own experience I can now concur that it's a powerful tool which I highly recommend to anyone who wants to see their goals grow into reality.

On 28 December 2014 I got a few hours away from the hustle and bustle and wrote down my goals. I cover the three main areas of my life: health and well-being, exercise and fitness and family and business goals, in that order. You may think it strange that family isn't first on the list; however, what I now understand is that unless I'm fit and healthy, I'm going to be no use to myself, my family or anyone else for that matter.

When writing down your goals it's important that the goals you're setting are achievable, but if you are to achieve true growth, they also must get you out of your comfort zone and significantly challenge you. When I finished goal-setting that day, there was one goal on the sheet that scared the living hell out of me: Ironman 2015. Among the nineteen other goals I'd written down, I challenged myself to complete – alive! – an Ironman in 2015. That was one hell of a task given the fact that I had only really learned to swim in the past fifteen months. How the hell would I swim 2.4 miles in the sea, cycle 112 miles on a bike and run a marathon, one after the other with no rest in between? It was a huge goal, a magnificent challenge and, for me, a life-changing moment. I was apprehensive and concerned that maybe this was just completely unrealistic. Major doubt set in and stayed with me for some time. Maybe I should have a think about this a little longer and get real. That little green man in my subconscious who I often referred to in my first book, *Attitude Is Everything*, was laughing his head off at me thinking I could actually complete an Ironman.

For those of you who have been following my story, you'll be aware that I ran my first marathon in 2011, Belfast City Marathon, and I ran to raise funds and awareness for Action MS. This was an incredibly difficult and ambitious challenge for me at that time; my MS was quite active and problematic to live with. Normal tasks like visiting the supermarket were more of a challenge. I was in a dark place, and managing that and all that goes with it while also training for a marathon was a tall order. The good news was that after four hours and thirty-six minutes I finished the marathon and got my medal. That was really the start of my relationship with adventure racing and also a defining moment for me in proving the importance of exercise in my recovery plan and in my ability to manage my multiple sclerosis.

Post Belfast City Marathon I focused on my training and committed myself to getting fitter and stronger and improving my diet and nutrition. I realised that if I was to have a chance of overcoming this illness, I had to change everything about my life. I recognised the power of exercise, adventures and the important role challenges could play if I was to keep on my path of recovery. In 2012 I ran the New York City Marathon, in 2013, Dublin Marathon and in 2014 I ran two – London and Dublin marathons. The buzz I was getting from smashing these challenges was tremendous, and, much better than that, I was aware of the hope I was giving to the MS community and others worldwide that despite living with a challenging illness like MS, it's still possible to be the master of your own destiny and live a very fulfilling life. The last few years have been incredible. I've received support from thousands of people across the world and have raised the profile of MS internationally. This is massively empowering and humbling at the same time, and is one of the main reasons why I continue to set myself challenges and goals every year.

In 2014 I thought it would be fantastic if I could get my body and mind in such a condition that I could complete a triathlon. The only problem was, although I could run and probably cycle – I hadn't cycled since I was a young boy, I couldn't swim the 750 metres needed to complete a sprint triathlon, the shortest and easiest triathlon of the lot. However, I thought that if I took a couple of swimming lessons, I might pick it up quickly enough, and then it would only be a matter of getting in the pool and practicing. And that's exactly what I did. After lessons in March 2014 and a bit of practicing, I entered my first sprint triathlon in June with five hundred other enthusiastic triathletes. If you haven't competed in triathlons or don't know much about them, I can tell you that there's an amazing buzz standing at the starter's gun. The spirit and camaraderie is tremendous, and I really felt a tingling in my stomach that morning in Derry. It was pissing out of the heavens, freezing cold, but still the atmosphere was fantastic. It was that morning that I fell in love with the sport and everything that goes with it. After one hour and forty-two minutes I crossed the finishing line to rapturous applause from the crowd. It was an amazing experience, and to top it off I was now officially a triathlete.

One of the things that stands out about a triathlon is the competitors. They represent every walk of life with one common denominator: they all have huge smiles on their faces throughout the race – it's incredible. Completing this race gave me a momentous faith in my convictions especially as I was able to swim almost half a mile in open water without stopping, which was something I never thought I'd be able to do. This was my first race and I was already hooked. I realised that if I just stuck with my plan, I could continue to get stronger and lead an adventurous and exciting life.

After setting my goals in 2014, I returned to the family and decided I would make an extra effort to enjoy the festive season this year, and, as it turned out, we had a great time together as a family. Lilyanna was four and young Conor one and a half and making serious progress. It's amazing having young children wake up on Christmas morning and run into the room to find Santa has come. I love family life, and my children have made a huge impact on me as a person and changed my life for the better. The break turned out to be just what the doctor ordered. I knew I needed to enjoy it as come January, post my goal session, I was very aware that I had to be extremely focused and disciplined if I was to have a chance of reaching my goals. I also had to prepare a plan of how I was going to actually complete an Ironman – Jesus Christ, how the hell was I going to do that? Having a couple of sprint triathlons under my belt was one thing, but completing an Ironman, well that was off the scale. Maybe it was too big a challenge? Maybe I needed to pull the horns in a little bit. After all, although my MS was under control for the most part, I still felt like crap at least seventy per cent of the time. How would I ever commit to the training program if I was having too many bad days? So many questions and I hadn't even started the bloody training. Aw well, I thought. I'll enjoy one last box of orange matchsticks with Lilyanna because after that I have to get the game-head on. That was the plan anyway.

CHAPTER 2

You can quit if you want, and no one will care.
But you will know the rest of your life.
JOHN COLLINS, IRONMAN CO-FOUNDER

Swim, Bike, Run

John Collins, a retired US navy officer, says he had no idea that someday the Ironman challenge he helped found in 1978 would be an international phenomenon. Collins and his family had participated in endurance sports for years, and it was at an award's banquet in Hawaii that he and some buddies rehashed their ongoing argument of who was in better shape: swimmers, runners or cyclists. The conversation progressed to a discussion around who of the three specialists would be first to finish a race that encompassed swimming, cycling and running. Collins suddenly stepped up to the microphone and announced his provisional plan for a race comprising all three sports. The first to finish would be the 'Ironman', a reference used for navy shipyard runners who could run twenty miles at the same pace as they would run two.

On the day of the race, 18 February 1978, fifteen competitors turned out. At the beginning of the race Collins handed each competitor a handout with a few simple rules. At the end it read: 'Swim 2.4 miles! Bike 112 miles! Run 26.2 miles! Brag for the rest of your life.' Three dropped out during the race and twelve finished.

Nearly forty years later and IRONMAN the brand has gone from strength to strength. In August 2015 Wanda Group, a leading Chinese private conglomerate, acquired the IRONMAN company for $650 million from Providence Equity Partners. This shows you the strength of the brand, the interest in the sport and that triathlon is in good health as one of the fastest growing sports in the world.

When I completed my first marathon in 2011 it was a tremendous feeling. It was a massive achievement for me, and it was the catalyst to my continuing interest in challenging myself physically through different adventures. Above all else, it gave me huge confidence, and I noticed that the more I trained and ate better, the stronger my mind and body became. At that time my MS was very active, but the more I looked after myself the better and stronger I felt. Slowly but surely, over time, I noticed a difference. This encouraged me to look for other people around the world who had made similar lifestyle changes, and guess what? My experience wasn't unique. Many others with similar philosophies were reporting comparable results. I knew that I needed to commit to this way of life if I was to have a chance of living the life I wanted while making sure my MS was kept under control. For me life is now all about playing the percentage game. I knew MS was a lifelong condition when I was diagnosed in 2007, but after my first marathon I also knew that if I continued with my plan, I could lead a very fulfilling and rewarding life. That first marathon was a major turning point for me as I realised for the first time that, against all odds, with the right plan and correct action, anything is possible. One of the things all dreamers and goal-setters will tell you is that when you set yourself goals and achieve them, it gives you so much self-belief – this is a hugely empowering feeling.

As I continued to challenge myself, I heard more and more people talking about triathlons. This is where it appeared to be at, and all I knew was that anyone who was doing a triathlon was fit, strong and, in general, quite tough. I searched the Internet to see if there was anyone competing in triathlons who had multiple sclerosis, and the truth was I couldn't find anyone. That spurred me on as I've always been one to step up to the plate and show some leadership – this was the right type of challenge at the right time in my life. It would be a powerful story if I could achieve this goal, and I knew it had the potential to inspire and empower others to start moving and dream again despite their difficulties. Swimming, cycling and running: the three arts of movement. If I could conquer all three, I knew this would help my well-being and also help me develop a robust mindset which would potentially benefit me in many other areas of my life.

In 2013 I completed my first triathlon in Derry. It was a sprint triathlon, and the perfect way to kick things off if you've an interest in this sport. Since then I've taken part in a grand total of five triathlons, so I'm by no means a newbie to the sport, and was completely aware of the jump in challenge by even considering a triathlete's holy grail in becoming an iron man. It was off the scale because there was so much to think about, so much training to undertake and it was also quite dangerous. I researched the event and very quickly became aware that not everyone who starts the race finishes it. This is a very sobering thought, and, in fact, over forty people in the last ten years have died taking part in triathlons in America alone. A lot of whom perish in the water for reasons including increased anxiety levels and heart attacks. As a very weak swimmer and someone who doesn't like being in water over my waist, I was starting to think this was a pretty silly idea. The truth was, this particular goal scared the living hell out of me. What were the chances of someone who was a novice triathlete with multiple sclerosis completing an Ironman in one piece? I wasn't too sure what the answer would be but I knew it was dangerous idea, and I have to admit I had serious doubts as to whether to proceed or call the whole thing off.

One of my mentors regularly states that if you're going to have goals, there must be at least one that scares you. I'm a fairly forensic type of person and I knew with the little research I had carried out that an Ironman was a dangerous thing to be considering and came with lots of risks. Would it bring on a relapse of my MS? What if something bad happened me? What if I died taking part? This was all very possible given the background research I had carried out, and it scared me. It's one thing to write goals over Christmas when you're looking to achieve personal growth; however, it's another matter altogether when you're writing goals that are very dangerous and could kill you if they're not carried out with caution. An Ironman takes you to the limit in every sense of the word, and there are no hiding places out there on the course. I had the complication of living with and trying to manage multiple sclerosis, and, on reflection, I knew this was probably a silly thing to be contemplating.

I approached this challenge in the same way I do anything in my life now. My next step was to get a plan in place, break it down in my head and take the appropriate action. This would give me a fighting chance of completing the challenge. If you don't have a plan in life, then ultimately you'll be living like a crisp bag in the wind, which doesn't get you very far. For an Ironman, a plan was not only crucial to survival, but also necessary. So many thoughts were going through my mind and I wasn't sure what to do or even where to start. One thing I did know was that if I was to achieve this goal, I needed to first of all enter a race. Because I hadn't done that, I did think I could just forget about it and do something else – maybe an ultra marathon – and just keep my head down. Nobody would know I'd chickened out, and maybe that was the more sensible thing to do in any case.

On Sunday, 3 January 2015, I booked my place in the Majorca Ironman on 26 September 2015. I couldn't pull out now the money was paid. What had I done? Was I wise? How on earth would I do this? All genuine questions, but the bottom line was I now needed to think about answering those questions over the weeks and months ahead. I knew from that night on that if I was to do this, I needed to condition my mind in such a way that I was going to cross the line. I needed to educate myself on every area of the race, understand the mental and physical demands and lastly, but most importantly, do what my friend Mr. Branson says – 'Just do it'. It took me a few days to get there mentally, but that's exactly what I decided to do.

I thought about how I was going to get my body in such shape that I could get over the finishing line in one piece come September. I wasn't trying to win the bloody thing, all I wanted to do was finish it, alive – and I'm not joking. The event was in nine months, so I had time to prepare for the race and kick-start my preparation. One of the first things I did was buy some books on the subject to help me get my head around all that was involved. With triathlons there is so much information to take on board and understand. To break it down and look at running, for example, there are numerous running books, coaches and loads of information out there to help you run better. It's the same for swimming and cycling, and if the truth be told, the whole thing is overwhelming because a lot of the information can be contradictory.

Outside of the three sports, there's lots of information, advice and opinions on nutrition and diet. Then there's the small matter of bike mechanics. Now I can ride a bike as well as any man; however, at that time, my last cycle was over twenty-five years ago on my BMX. I didn't even like cycling, and out of the three sports it was the one I was mentally struggling with. For some time I failed to understand how I could get through a 112-mile bike ride. I was pretty confident I could manage it in a car, but a bike? It just didn't sound like much fun to me or even normal behavior, but I was all too aware that it had to be done, so I needed to not only get my head around it but also work out how I was going to physically overcome that part of the Ironman. As I was thinking about how I would do this, a Eureka moment occurred: since my diagnosis in 2007 I had raised many thousands of pounds for the Multiple Sclerosis Society, and through my website, book, blogs and my adventures I had done quite a bit to increase the profile of the condition worldwide. At that moment I came up with six events, including marathons and triathlons, that would be central to my training plan.

My Plan of Action

My first event would be the Belfast City Marathon in May 2015 and my second event would be a few weeks later, the Walled City Marathon in Derry. I felt that if I got those two marathons in early, that would give my body a great platform to build from and get stronger. Over the summer months I then planned to compete in the Derry Sprint Triathlon in June and the Belfast Olympic Triathlon in July. In August I would up my game and compete in Ireland's first ever IRONMAN-branded event in the Dublin 70.3 race. Post that, if I was still in one piece, I would be in great shape for Alcúdia on 26 September. I started to get very excited about the challenge now because I knew that if I could get through the first five events and remain injury free, I would have a great chance of achieving my goal in becoming an iron man.

Brilliant. Now that I had the plan worked out, all I needed to do was brand it up and check that the MS Society would be ok with me primarily completing my challenge to raise funds for them but also using it to raise the profile of MS across the world. After a meeting with the local branch director, I got the full backing of the team and officially launched my Against All Odds campaign in March 2015. The twist in the tale, of course, was that I would be doing all six events in twenty weeks, so I certainly wasn't planning on hanging about.

I love thinking, being creative and challenging myself, and I felt there was something special about my campaign. I also felt that it would reach out to people and they would see that this was a genuinely tough program and huge effort would be required to accomplish it. I hoped that people would put their hands in their pockets and sponsor me, raising some much-needed funding for MS research.

Great. I was on fire and buzzing with excitement. I had the whole thing worked out: I was going to do six events in twenty weeks and raise a load of money for the MS Society – fantastic. Although the events I had set myself were quite tough, I had a feeling I could complete them all if I stuck to my plan. The only thing I needed to do now was pull together a training plan with a start date and take it from there.

One of the great things about the Internet is that it has all the information you need on any subject at the touch of a button, including Ironman. It's a huge sport and one of the fastest-growing brands in the world, so there's a wealth of information available. After some initial research I came across what looked to be the book for me: *Iron Fit* by Don Fink, an internationally known triathlete coach. Over the years Fink has trained thousands of athletes with outstanding success stories. I thought he was the man for me and so immediately ordered a copy of his book. The night *Iron Fit* arrived, I got stuck in. I knew after a few pages it was the book for me because it was easy to read and the chapters flowed. It covered everything I needed to know about triathlons and gave three options of training plans so I could pick the plan that suited me best. Each training plan lasted for thirty weeks and I could choose from the just-finish program (I liked the sound of that), the intermediate program and the competitive program. Each program was, for the most part, the same and distinguished only by the amount of hours training involved. Obviously the just-finish program had the least amount of training with a maximum of ten hours per week. The intermediate program went up to fifteen hours per week and the competitive program maxed out at twenty hours per week at its toughest point.

I really needed to give this some thought as I had to take into account my young family, my wife and my all-consuming business. I needed to make sure that this new training program had a limited effect, if any, on the other important aspects of my life. I also knew that if I was to do this, I needed to commit to a program and stick with it; it would be far too dangerous to go into this campaign half-heartedly. It needed maximum commitment and planning if I wanted to succeed in my six chosen events. As I studied Fink's book, I focused on the intermediate program because it appeared to be something I could work with. I planned to train in the gym every lunchtime, and at the weekend get in a few more hours out on the roads. I was used to training at this point, and, ever ambitious, I decided to run with the intermediate program.

Around the start of February I wanted to get in the zone and prepare myself mentally for the months of training that lay ahead because an Ironman is as much a mental challenge as it is physical, as many people will testify. One thing I noticed – and I still get this – is that when I first told people what was involved, they looked at me as if I had horns coming out of my head for even considering such an extreme challenge, but it was imperative I educated myself around what was involved, armed myself with as much information as possible and stuck to the plan. And that was what I intended to do. What I really needed now was a dose of inspiration, and who better to look to than Chrissie Wellington? Chrissie, an English lady, is an Ironman legend and I encourage you to read her book, *A Life Without Limits: A World Champion's Journey*. In October 2007, at thirty years of age and virtually unknown in Ironman, Chrissie went on to win the Ironman World Championship in Hawaii. The fascinating thing about Chrissie's story is that nine months earlier she had been a civil servant working in her native England – an incredible rise and an incredible achievement from a remarkable lady.

Over the years, one thing that has really helped me when I'm down is finding other people across the world who, like me, are also facing adversity in their own lives. Try it. For me, it's incredible to hear some of the stories out there, and I often say to people that it's healthy to find people who inspire you to achieve your own goals. In fact, I would go so far as to say that it's a necessity.

A few days after I read Chrissie's book, my training partner and good buddy, Gerard McAdorey (Gmac), handed me *Iron War*; a fascinating book that sets out the rivalry between two of Ironman's greatest legends, Dave Scott and Mark Allen. These two books, along with some others, set the foundations for me to expand my mind to believe the impossible was possible. I knew the size of the challenge I had set myself, but I was also very excited about the prospect of my Against All Odds campaign, and I knew that if I stuck with Don Fink's thirty-week training plan, ate the right food and stayed injury free, the Ironman dream was well and truly alive.

CHAPTER 3

To hell with circumstances; I create opportunities.
BRUCE LEE

Dealing with the Unexpected

Sitting in the neurologist's chair in 2007 and hearing the words, 'Conor, you have multiple sclerosis, and you will have it for the rest of your life,' my world fell in around me. Although I had been really sick since my first attack in Mauritius twelve months previous, to my own mind I went to my neurologist that day to be told that I was fine and that this whole health-scare shenanigans would pass. Instead, I left that small, stuffy office in pieces and made the lonely walk to my car, opened the door and got in before the tears started to roll down my cheeks. I must have sat there staring out the windscreen completely devastated and totally shattered for the next half hour. At twenty-eight years of age, all my dreams were now in tatters. How could this be? Why was this happening to me? I had so many questions and no answers whatsoever. I felt lonely, isolated, afraid and lost; not a nice place to be at all. If I'm honest with myself, my diagnosis wasn't a complete shock. Over the previous twelve months I had had lots of symptoms that had made my life hell, and my gut instinct was telling me that there was a strong possibility I had MS. However, ever the optimist, it wasn't until Mr. Watt told me to my face that beautiful morning that I believed it to be the case. What a nightmare. And I knew one thing: from that day on my life was going to change.

Early Days

From a young boy I was always curious, mischievous and pushing myself forward. I had an inbuilt drive to be the best at anything I did, and from an early age developed a competitive and combative personality. I enjoyed most sports but football was my first love. I've worked out that by the age of eleven I had over five thousand hours of practice under my belt having never been without a ball from the age of three. I've since come to understand that you're considered an expert in your field once you've accumulated ten thousand hours of practice or study, so at eleven years of age I was well on my way to being very handy at football.

I always loved a challenge, and one of my first memories of a sporting battle was in primary seven at a football blitz that comprised many of the local primary schools in the country. My teacher at the time, and one of the first people who really believed in me, Mr. Cullen, made me captain and I ended up being the team's talisman throughout the tournament and in what turned out to be a great day creating fantastic lifelong memories for me. We beat most of the schools quite easily because of our strong team, but there was one rival school from a neighboring village that was the team to beat. Mr. Cullen had watched them and they had one player in particular who was pretty much winning all of their games for them. Before the final Mr. Cullen told me that I would be marking this guy, and although he was a foot (at least) taller than me and appeared stronger, I was to keep moving and make sure he was running after me and not the other way round. The good news is that this was a great decision by the manger as I had a terrific final scoring a couple of goals and a few points to finish with the man-of-the-match trophy and, to cap the day off, the player of the tournament. Many years after that tournament, the guy I was asked to mark reminded me of how well I played that day. I absolutely loved scoring goals and taking people on, and I knew that with all the hours of practice in my backyard, I was good at football.

Throughout my younger years I continued to excel at football – both soccer and Gaelic. I loved the competitive nature of the sport, the highs and the lows and all the banter that goes with it. I also believe that it was the company I kept and the discipline of sport in my formative years that made a real impact on me as a person and which helped sow the seeds of many of my characteristics and gave me the platform to be the person I am today. As I've got older and more experienced, one thing I've realized is that in life there will always be unexpected obstacles; these are the facts of life and are simply unavoidable. Lots of things have happened in my life that I found very difficult to deal with: failing the eleven-plus, failing my driving test (twice) and being turned down for a professional football contract in England, to name a few, but being diagnosed with multiple sclerosis at twenty-eight was certainly not something I wanted for my life. I had many hopes, dreams and plans as a young man and always wanted to better myself, so this disease was most unwelcome. I now believe that when the unexpected comes, particularly something very serious, you react in one of two ways: you either let it dominate, control and destroy you, or you take the negative energy and turn it into a positive vibe and ultimately use it to make you stronger. This is easier said than done, and in my own situation it took me four years to work out how I was going to deal with my MS and change a difficult, negative experience into a more positive one.

From 2006 to 2010 I switched off, gave up and lost all hope. I felt myself go steadily downhill, at times losing the will to live. It was a desperate few years. Then, one day, I came across two people who inspired me to get my act together and fight back, and guess what? That's what I did. I started the long road of recovery which continues every day. This is what is great about adversity – whenever something bad happens, there's always some good to come out of it. In 2011, when I finally got my act together and my plan in place, I used all the negative energy of the last few years to get me round Belfast City Marathon, my first marathon. It was an incredible experience and one that I thought was impossible given my health status. How wrong was I?

The Mind

Although I knew in my own head that an Ironman was going to be incredibly difficult, from the moment I wrote the goal on my page, I started to work on my subconscious mind to persuade it that this dream was possible.

We all have two minds: the conscious and the subconscious. The conscious mind is the polite chap who is agreeable, often direct and the one who could pass himself in any crowd. It can be talked round even when at first it's not so sure because it's always keen to fit in and is impulsive by its very nature. If you're asked to do a bungee jump tomorrow morning at ten, it's likely that your conscious mind will immediately (if you're like me) tell you to catch yourself on. However, after half an hour of your friends telling you it's not so bad and that the oldest person to do one is ninety-seven and he jumps three times a week, the conscious mind will likely come round and you may find yourself agreeing to jump after all. But the subconscious mind is a different operation altogether. It's the subconscious mind that performs almost five million exercises per second to keep everything in the human body functioning properly. The subconscious is the boss, the master and whatever it says goes. The interesting thing is that the subconscious mind can't distinguish between what is real and what isn't, but it has a view on everything. To achieve goals and make progress in life, you have to know how the subconscious mind works, and, more importantly, how to get it to change its view on things and do what your conscious mind wants it to do. This can be very difficult, and it was especially so at the beginning of this journey; however, it is achievable.

Over the last number of years, as I continue to stick to my plan, I've talked directly to my subconscious mind. I've been able to get a firm grip of its thoughts which has been a huge benefit in dealing with the challenges in my life and the goals I continue to set myself. This takes constant work and effort but once mastered can be tremendously rewarding and empowering. With the Ironman it was straightforward: my conscious mind wanted to do the race and believed I could do it, but my subconscious was shouting at the top of its voice, 'Conor, you have absolutely no chance of completing this event – you can barely swim, for fuck's sake.'

The truth is, this is a very difficult situation to be in, but it happens to all of us a lot of the time. You want to change your career, maybe you hate your job and decide to set up your own business just like I did, but your subconscious mind is telling you it's totally impossible and it's best you stay put. For two years I knew what I wanted to do: work for myself, and although my conscious mind agreed, my subconscious mind told me it would never happen, that I wasn't ready, that I would fail. The list of negative thoughts and feelings went on and on and on. At that time I educated myself on what was involved and began convincing my subconscious that I could actually do it, that I was strong enough and that I would be successful. After two years of personal development and studying hard on my business plan, I convinced myself that I could do it and set up the GDP Partnership.

An Ironman was no different. I needed to up my game, get with the program and see what was involved with this challenge. I knew it was bloody tough – it's recognised as one of the hardest sports known to man, but so what? Life's tough. So instead of moaning about how hard it was going to be, I focused on how I was going to smash it – yes, smash it.

Training Plan

Don Fink's book was a good way to start convincing my subconscious mind that an Ironman was an achievable goal. Reading through the first sections of the book, and after giving it some thought, I worked out that the intermediate program was the best training plan for me. Who the hell wants to 'just finish' an Ironman? Why bother? I thought. If I did 'just finish', fantastic, but I was going to condition my mind over the next thirty weeks to cross the line stronger than 'just finish'.

The thirty-week program is broken into three ten-week segments. The base phase in weeks one to ten is to build strength and conditioning. It begins with only six hours of training in week one: two hours in each sport and eight sessions in total – three on the bike, three runs and two swims. From there training builds for an hour each week for three weeks and then decreases by an hour every fourth week. Come week ten there are a total of eleven hours of training over eight sessions. The swim training comprises drills that it asks you to increase time wise and in terms of metres covered over the first twelve weeks before reducing accordingly. The long bike starting in week one lasts an hour and builds to three hours by week ten. The long run starts at forty-five minutes in week one and is one and a half hours by week ten.

The base phase averages about eight and a half hours per week. The more I got into it and read through what was required, the more I could feel my mind expand and recognise what I could potentially achieve. I genu-inely think that my subconscious was already believing that my challenge was achievable because I believed I could manage this training program. This was a turning point for me regarding the six events that lay ahead and my belief that I could actually complete them.

Weeks eleven to twenty are the build phase with eleven hours training in week eleven climbing to twelve and a half hours in week nineteen. Swim sessions increase from two to three hours, the long bike increases to four hours and the long run builds to two hours. There are a couple of higher in-tensity sessions thrown in for good measure, and in general the effort level, training times and pressure increases.

Weeks twenty-one to thirty are the peak phase. This phase begins with a half Ironman which worked well for me as I had one in for 9 August in Dublin – happy days. There is then an intense five-week program followed by a three-week pre-race tapering off which finishes with the Ironman itself.

Weekly training at week twenty-one starts at thirteen hours and increases to fifteen hours at week twenty-five. By week twenty-seven it drops back to thirteen hours to give you time to get yourself physically and mentally ready for the big one. Overall this phase averages out at thirteen hours training per week which I thought achievable.

Over the next few weeks I studied this plan, and the more I thought about it the more I believed I could actually do it. With each book I read and the more research I did, the more I felt my subconscious mind coming round to the possibility of me achieving my dream. Over time I visualised myself crossing the finishing line and began to believe that I was going to do this. In my experience, the hardest part of a physical challenge is often committing to it in the first place. If you agree to a training program, get your trainers on and get out there, most things tend to fall into place. A friend told me that an Ironman is seventy per cent mental ability and thirty per cent physical; the results from my research convinced me that this was the case. My Ironman journey was now getting incredibly exciting.

The intermediate plan was perfect for me, and I knew if I could stick to it (why couldn't I, with a maximum of fifteen hours per week?), then I would get this bloody thing done. How cool would that be? And what an achievement. I was beginning to get a buzz about the challenge I had set myself, and also at this time my story was starting to get some traction with elements of the media, with some journalists taking an interest (a few of them questioned my sanity, which was probably fair enough). In my world, though, the more people who doubted my sanity and doubted that I could do this, the more determined and focused I became.

One thing I needed to sort out fast was my structure – how was I going to manage everything that was going on in my life and also train for an Ironman? When I started my training program in March, I was running a successful and demanding business. By then the company had been trading a few years and was thriving. I had eight staff to look after along with a myriad of day-to-day situations that need sorting when you run your own company, so I needed to get a plan in place quickly. The other matter to take into account was that I had a young family to think of, and it's pointless coming up with challenges and goals which have a negative impact on family life. I had a lot to think about but was still confident I could pull this off without having a detrimental effect on the important areas in my life. Ultimately, I would have to become seriously well-organised – regimented is probably a better way to describe it – but if I could get a plan in place that suited my day to day life, I could pull this off.

My children were very young, so my initial plan was to train at lunchtime in the gym through the week; this then wouldn't interfere with my work or home life. I could work the weekend's fine if I got up at stupid o'clock because I only needed a maximum of a few hours training on Saturdays and Sundays. If I was up and at it before Lilyanna and Conor were awake, they wouldn't be missing out.

Most people I talk to about Ironman think it's an amazing challenge, and many aspire to do an Ironman at some point, but one of the first excuses people come up with is that they're too busy and don't have the time to train. Even for a half-marathon people find it hard to fit in training as they're busy with work, family commitments and looking after the goldfish. This is one of the biggest cop outs of all time, and I'd prefer people told the truth and said they didn't have the desire to do it, didn't have the balls to do it, couldn't be arsed with the training or whatever the real reason is. I'd bet you a pound that if most were honest, they couldn't be bothered stepping out of their comfort zone. This is actually quite sad as far too many people never realise their full potential because they don't push themselves out of their comfort zone. If I can train for an Ironman, bring up a young family, deal with multiple sclerosis and run a business, then you can do it too. The important point being, you have to *want* to do something no matter what it is. Your *why* must be strong enough for you to do whatever is necessary to achieve the result you want. I now had so many reasons to complete my Ironman and I was looking forward to getting stuck in.

CHAPTER 4

I'm always looking to make choices that get me out
of my comfort zone. For as long as you are always
uncomfortable, you will always be growing.
CONOR DEVINE

Against All Odds

I worked my way through *Iron Fit* and other popular Ironman books trying
to glean as much information as possible. In the process I gained an understanding of just how special the event was that I had committed to. I still
had to pinch myself to make sure this was really happening. I also had the
small matter of dealing with my daily MS symptoms not to mention sticking to my training program, running my business and family life too.

Although my MS was under control for the most part, I still felt rough
a lot of the time. To the naked eye people can't tell there is a problem because much of the internal damage MS causes, such as the destruction of
nerve endings, is invisible. This gives me a range of debilitating symptoms,
one of which is feeling crap day to day. Thankfully though, in the last number of years I've experienced many more good days than bad, which is a
direct response to the recovery plan I have been sticking rigidly to.

MS is a complex condition officially affecting over 2.5 million people
worldwide (and many more unofficially), and, as the saying goes, no two

people are affected in the same way. It's well-documented that there are over fifty different symptoms of MS, and between 2006 and 2010 I experienced over twenty of these manifestations every day. My main symptoms were vertigo, balance problems, throat issues, head pain and electric-shock sensations racing through my body that focused on the backs of my knees and my chest – great craic altogether. Many days were a struggle to even get out of bed never mind think about going for a short run; however, thankfully, since I implemented my three-point plan in 2010, my symptoms have steadily settled to a level that, for the most part, are manageable, and as a result I'm fortunate to lead a normal, active life. The caveat here is that I work tremendously hard on my health and well-being so that I can manage my MS. Sure it's hard work being disciplined enough to stick to the plan and keep on track, but the benefits I'm experiencing now makes all the effort over the last few years worthwhile.

Attitude is Everything, my first book, documents my MS journey, my three-point plan and my recovery, but what follows here is an overview of my personal plan which has put me on the road to recovery.

(1) Medication
After my diagnosis in 2007 I was offered a disease-modifying drug. The drugs that are available to MS patients have been proven to prevent relapses by up to thirty per cent, and at that time I felt it was the right thing to do, so I decided on Copaxone, and until April 2016 – nine years later – I injected every day. I am now drug-free as I have made so much progress in the last few years that I now don't feel the need to administer Copaxone. This has been an incredible development for me and from a mindset point of view has had a hugely positive impact.

(2) Food and Exercise
Over the last few years I've steadily migrated away from a Westernised diet of processed, dairy-riddled food to a diet of real and plant-based foods.

This has been a journey in itself and one that I foresee myself continuing on. It's hugely frustrating for me as a MS patient that there continues to be a global disconnect between combining conventional medicine with unconventional methods to benefit, manage, and in many cases reverse, MS and other illnesses. Clearly the medical data and the clinical trials from the last twenty years have proven that MS patients should include medication in their recovery plans; however, there is now similar evidence-based trials available that set out the benefits of adopting the right nutritional plan coupled with exercise. For the last few years I've had the pleasure of addressing many high-level MS conferences across Europe where the audience is normally restricted to pharmaceutical companies and medical professionals. I always take the opportunity to raise this matter, and, thankfully, as time progresses there is an acknowledgement that there is a place for diet and exercise as well as conventional medicine. I now truly believe that a huge part of my remarkable recovery is down to the food I've been eating in the last few years and my energetic exercise regime.

(3) Personal Development

Personal development is a huge area which is a little complex to explain and, for some, understandably, a little complex to understand exactly how it can help you progress in life if embraced correctly. I think the simplest way to describe this to you is to say that I made a conscious decision to embrace my own personal development and in doing so allowed myself to take control of my thoughts, my MS, my education of life, dealing with challenges and trying to understand how I can become a better version of me. It's probably best you read the last few lines again, and maybe just one more time, to be completely clear on the matter.

It's a very fulfilling, authentic way to engage in life, and if I want to continue to prosper, I feel this is a lifetime commitment. It requires a huge amount of effort, dedication and discipline but it pays dividends. If you can get your mind in the right place with personal development, I believe everything else will look after itself.

As a child I had a precious and enjoyable upbringing. My parents worked round the clock to ensure my siblings and I had all we needed, and I did well academically achieving my degree in estate management from the University of Ulster in 2002. But it took me twenty-eight years to hear the words 'personal development' from one of my teachers. Why? My own view is that our schooling system is wrong. We are conditioned from a young age to do well at school, go to university, get a degree and a job in a PLC and make its directors and shareholders a shedload of money. Well, I disagree with that philosophy, instead preferring a system that teaches and conditions our children to think for themselves, be entrepreneurs and problem-solvers with aspirations of owning and building their own businesses. I think this is a hard nut to crack, but I know what I'll be doing with my own children to fill the vacuum.

You may think I'm straying from the subject here, and you may even question what the hell this has got to do with Ironman and developing an iron mind; however, personal development has changed my life and my future. It brought me hope and belief at my lowest point that absolutely everything was possible. I read Napoleon Hill's book, *Think and Grow Rich*, in 2011, and every year since I've been studying and reviewing his seventeen principles of success. It's an amazing piece of work which has helped me take control of my conscious and subconscious mind and I would encourage you to read it. Look what happened when I applied the first of Napoleon's thirteen principles: I controlled my thoughts, got a plan on paper, had a definite purpose and applied the right action. The next thing I knew, I was doing an Ironman! I rest my case.

At Christmas 2014, what I wanted to achieve was primarily my Ironman goal, but with the amount of effort I was going to be putting in I really wanted to enjoy the process too. I decided that the best way to do that was to take part in as many events as physically possible and genuinely try and love every moment. It was this mindset that created my Against All Odds campaign which I referred to in chapter two.

I consider myself an MS advocate raising the profile of multiple sclerosis worldwide through my website, blog posts, social networking, adventures and events. It's hugely important to me and empowering to know that through my actions I can help and inspire people who suffer from MS and other conditions or illnesses. This is what I refer to as my definite of purpose, and it's something I'm passionate about. I knew there was a good chance my Ironman would get some profile as not many MS'ers in the world undertake such an insane challenge, and I also knew that, if positioned correctly, my ambitious Against all Odds campaign would have the potential to go far and wide to raise awareness of MS and a lot of cash for my charity.

Six in Twenty Weeks

Six events in twenty weeks: two triathlons, two marathons, a half Ironman and a full Ironman – that was one hell of a task to complete, and the more people who found out about it, the more money that was going into my Just Giving account; I wasn't sure if this was an acknowledgement of how tough the task was or whether it was in recognition of my insanity. The Against All Odds campaign that came to me one evening at home as I tried to work out what would both capture people's imaginations and take me out of my comfort zone was certainly now ticking those boxes, and I knew that the first five events would give me a buffer to the Ironman and allow me to focus on the individual events one at a time as opposed to freaking out about the biggie in just over six months' time.

There was a lot going on in my mind, and, although great to look at on paper, I was slightly concerned with the challenge I had set myself. It wasn't that I thought I couldn't do it, it was more from an injury point of view – how could I put my body through so much stress and not pick up a strain which could ultimately put an end to the main goal in September? There were six big races ahead of me, and this, coupled with an intensive training program, was a big ask which didn't leave a lot of room for the rest I was going to need if I was to get through the next number of months, something I had neglected to think about. I only average six hours' sleep a night at best, so rest is really a bit of a luxury.

Competing in an Ironman is one thing, but two marathons, two triathlons and a half Ironman for preparation – was that wise? I was too committed at this point, and how I sold it to my subconscious was that if I could get through the training program in one piece, take it handy round each event, then I would be bang on for Majorca. The more I looked at it, the more ingenious I thought it was – it was brilliant. Now all I had to do was get to work. The plan was constructed, so the next thing I needed was to see my training and events scheduled on a calendar so that I was well-prepared and could visualise my entire program right through to the finishing line in Majorca. In early February my new wall planner arrived and I wrote in the six events and got it up on the wall. This was all getting very real. I was due to start Fink's thirty-week program shortly, and, although it was only February and I still had a few weeks off, I decided to start training every day, a mix of running, swimming and cycling – with a rest day on a Sunday.

The reality is I'm not a good swimmer at all. In fact, I would say I'm very weak, but I knew that if I kept getting in the pool, kept watching some swim technique videos on YouTube and kept studying the sport, I would improve – after all, it's not rocket science, is it? And guess what? That's exactly what happened over the next few months. I've never had any real love for cycling. I've often thought it pointless and at times still struggle to see how anyone could find it remotely exciting. To be fair though, I recognised that it was a great way to exercise and I found that in the first few weeks of training if you have a mate who has decent chat, then cycling is actually not a bad way to unwind and improve your mental health and your overall well-being. As time progressed my view on cycling changed for the better, but early on I definitely wouldn't have described myself as a good cyclist or someone who enjoyed cycling by any stretch. More accurately, I was shit at cycling and found it extremely boring as well as physically challenging.

Fink's thirty-week program kicked off, and I was really excited with how it was panning out. One of my motivations for doing this bloody thing was that I knew I would get into great shape, and the health and well-being benefits would be incredible. To actually be fit enough to train six days a week for an Ironman nine years after being diagnosed with MS – what a great achievement. It was such a good feeling, as if my subconscious was talking to my conscious mind and reminding it how strong and healthy I was.

Illness is a terrible thing to deal with, and if it goes so far as to take over your mind, then it will ultimately kill you. On the brink of starting an intensive training program, I was feeling good about myself, and, more so, thankful that my health was under control. I was confident this would continue and my mindset would get stronger. Yes, this was just what the doctor ordered.

Belfast City Marathon

With four weeks to go to the Belfast City Marathon, I appeared to be on schedule working my way through my training program at my leisure. However, as I was starting to think this was all rather manageable, disaster struck. I woke up on Monday, 6 April 2015 feeling really rough. Having lived with MS for over nine years, I can normally tell by eleven in the morning what kind of a day I'll have. On a bad day it hits me an hour after I get up, usually on my way into work. A really sick feeling comes over me and the energy drains from my body. All I want to do is go home, pull the duvet over my head and not wake up until the feeling goes away. I'll be honest with you, it's maybe not the cleverest thing to do but I've never actually done that, especially since I work for myself; I have to go into work, run the business and look after staff among the hundreds of other things needing done. Anyone who runs their own business will understand.

'Fuck right off,' I shouted in the empty car. 'I'm training for an Ironman and have a marathon in just over four weeks. I don't need this shit now.'

I hoped the feeling would pass in a few hours but unfortunately it continued to the Friday of the same week, which meant that, yes, I had a shit week health-wise, but, more importantly, I wasn't able to train. If this was a sign of things to come, I'd best call the whole thing off right now. I was annoyed that I may not be able to complete the challenge for which people were donating their hard-earned cash. I was in a fix, totally aware that my MS, although under control for the most part, was extremely unpredictable. It's upsetting at the best of times, and I'm not sure I'll ever get used to the crappy feeling when it flares up, but somewhere within me I got the strength to stay calm with the thought that tomorrow brings another day and another opportunity. The following week I felt a little better because the vertigo and dizziness had stopped. I wasn't one hundred per cent, far from it, but I was well enough to get back in the pool, back out on the road and also to hit the pedals. Apart from that time when I was unwell, my training program was working for me; it was good program and I enjoyed it. It was the first time in my life I had followed a professional training program and it was uplifting.

The second week of April passed by fine and I stuck with the training program for the most part. However, the following week was another wipe out as unfortunately my MS symptoms had reared their head again and were now causing me real problems. Funny how for the first three months of the year I was doing quite well, but now that I was training regularly I felt like crap again. This was really pissing me off and my morale was quite low. Each time this happens I always try to join the dots myself as I get little help from the medical team, and MS is such a complex, individual condition. A pattern I've noticed is that whenever I pick up a flu, for example, it hits me like a tonne of bricks, and at the beginning of April there was a wicked flu doing the rounds which unfortunately I had contracted and was now struggling to shake off. Each November I get the flu jab because my immune system needs as much help as it can get, but with over 220 different types of flu, it doesn't protect me against them all. Unluckily, I was now under the weather big time with dizziness and an overall shit feeling stopping me from training altogether. The Belfast City Marathon was only two weeks away and I genuinely wasn't sure if I was going to make the starting line. That would be disastrous for me. I thought about saving myself the embarrassment and cancelling the whole campaign, things were that bad.

On Monday, 4 May 2015, I lined up at the starter's gun for the Belfast City Marathon with my loyal running buddy, agony aunt and great friend, Gmac. It was a terrific morning in Belfast with the crowds super excited and thousands of runners ready to take on the 26.2 mile race. The build-up and training had been a catastrophe for me as I'd missed three weeks of training in April, but I had got out a few days the previous week and my plan was to simply finish the race with a smile and no injuries.

The marathon itself was, as ever, one of colour, atmosphere and excitement – that's the very least marathons bring to a city – and there was a feeling of well-being and gratefulness. The weather played an important role and we were lucky that the sun was out and everyone was in good form. After twenty-odd miles I was feeling good given my preparation over the previous month, but I've ran enough marathons to know that a good feeling can go in an instant and it wasn't too far past mile twenty that this happened. Sure enough, from mile twenty-one I went quickly downhill. My legs ached, my feet were sore and muscles all over my body started to cramp. I knew my pains were from my lack of training as there's one thing I've learned with previous races: you can't fool a marathon.

At mile twenty-four I was really struggling and actually felt quite sick. I was now running ten-plus minute miles, and, although I'm no Mo Farah, I normally like to canter along knocking out eight-and-a-half-minute miles; I was exhausted, sore and overcome with negativity. At mile twenty-five I saw Brenda from the MS Society and some of her gang. Seeing them reminded me why I was running the marathon in the first place and it gave me a pick-me-up … for all of a millisecond. One foot in front of the other, one foot in front of the other, one foot in front of the other became my mantra to the finishing line. Coming into Ormeau Park for the last half mile I was completely drained and wanted nothing more than to lie down. The only thing I thought about was how the hell I was going to complete an Ironman if I could hardly run a bloody marathon. With that thought in mind, and although barely able to speak, I crossed the finishing line and collected my second Belfast City Marathon medal. The clock read 4hr 36min, a slow time for me and way over what I had hoped to finish in, but I heard my subconscious whisper, 'Hang on a minute, Conor. You only wanted to finish, remember? Don't be so hard on yourself.'

As I walked along the recovery area, I was greeted by my five-year-old princess, Lilyanna, who handed me a ninety-nine with chocolate sprinkles and strawberry sauce – what a superstar. I barely had the energy to eat it but I gave it a good go. I remembered the goal I had set myself at the starting line – just finish the race with a smile and no injuries – so I tried my best to smile, but if truth be told, it was very hard. My young son, Conor Junior, was also at the finishing line to greet me, and just seeing him made it much easier to smile and be very grateful for what I had achieved despite the circumstances. So another marathon was in the bag: six in five years. Not bad for someone living with multiple sclerosis. At that point I lifted my arm and patted myself on the back and said to myself, 'Well done, Conor. You're off and running, sir. The dream is alive.'

CHAPTER 5

Let food be thy medicine and medicine be thy food.

Hippocrates

Food

One of the objectives for me writing this book was to let you into my life and show you how I achieved my Ironman dream despite the challenges I faced. As I've said before, an Ironman is seventy per cent mental ability and thirty percent physical. I know that if you can develop an iron mindset where you commit to a training program and believe you can achieve your goal, you will become the Ironman you aspire to be. Food and nutrition are hugely important topics not just for adventure racing but for all round health and well-being, and they played their part in helping me achieve my Ironman goal. Hopefully by the end of this chapter you'll have a better understanding of food and nutrition and how I fuelled myself before, during and after Ironman Majorca.

Some might say I'm one of the luckier ones in life because for most of the last thirty-eight years I ate whatever I wanted. My diet was healthy enough – I wasn't a health freak by any stretch but I did try to put healthy, or what I thought was healthy, food in my body, and as I came from a sporting background and exercised an average of three times a week, I never had a problem with my weight. Around 2010, as I was putting my plan together to fight against my MS, I got a huge wake-up call when I took a closer look at what I was eating. On reflection, if I'm honest with you, my diet wasn't actually all that healthy. Looking back I'd say it was pretty awful. Processed foods accounted for a large percentage of the food I'd eaten until 2010. I now know these to be unhealthy, but back then I never paid much attention to what I was putting in my body. I got away with it for so long because of my active lifestyle; however, who knows if it's come back to haunt me now that I'm living with MS. It wasn't until three years after I was diagnosed, in 2010, that I was forced to think more clearly about the food I was putting into the shopping trolley and subsequently into my body.

I'm not a doctor, nutritionist or pharmacist, but I am someone who was diagnosed with multiple sclerosis in 2007, and who can look back now and see that I fuelled my body with unhealthy food. Since 2010 I've become very interested in food as a way to optimise my well-being and enhance my performance levels in whatever I ask my body to do. Let me ask you a question. Take a moment and reflect on this: do I remind you of anyone? Maybe yourself? How many people go from day to day eating the same old crap, feeling tired and lethargic, picking up colds and flus, getting sick and finding it hard to make any real progress with themselves and life in general? I would say a fair percentage of people, and definitely most of those whom I've come into contact with.

Triathlon

During a triathlon race nutrition is very important, as if you haven't enough fuel in your body, you won't get to the finish line. There are hundreds of books out there willing to give you all sorts of advice around food: what you should and shouldn't be eating, your protein and carbohydrate requirements, how best to hydrate yourself, train and rest – the whole area is overwhelming. How I negotiated it to find my optimum food plan was by working off recommendations and trying the available options. In simple terms, it's about trial and error and educating yourself on what works best for your body. I tested different nutritional plans throughout my training and when competing until I came across a combination that felt right for me and which got me home and hosed in good order. There's little to be gained by reinventing the wheel, so I spoke to others to see what worked for them and was sensible in my approach to my personal circumstances.

I was helped along the way by Dr. Terry Wahls, a neurologist and clinical professor of medicine at the University of Iowa. She's held in high esteem by the medical profession and was the perfect point of entry for me to try and understand what I should and shouldn't be eating Monday to Sunday. One of the primary reasons I was drawn to Dr. Wahls is that she was diagnosed with relapsing remitting multiple sclerosis in 2000, which intrigued me. By 2003 she had deteriorated to secondary progressive multiple sclerosis and underwent chemotherapy in an attempt to slow the disease and began to use a tilt-recline wheelchair because of weakness in her back muscles. Over time Dr. Wahls decline continued, and she became bedridden by MS. She figured out that unless something changed very quickly, her future was grim. Left with little choice, she took the decision to stop medication and instead searched for vitamins and supplements that helped with any kind of progressive brain disorder. She found nutrients complementary to brain health and began taking them as supplements. Incredibly, the steepness of her decline slowed and her MS plateaued – what a turnaround. In December 2007 she documented The Wahls Protocol, her own diet and roadmap to recovery. The results were phenomenal: within one year she was able to walk without a stick and complete an eighteen-mile bike ride – what an incredible rehabilitation.

Dr. Wahls' work has greatly influenced my recovery and my thoughts around food and its connection to well-being, and, furthermore, you don't have to be suffering from multiple sclerosis to benefit from Dr. Wahls' knowledge on food and its connection to well-being. She has had a profound effect on me and is the reason I initially looked at the food I ate and how I refueled my body. I encourage you to look at her TEDx talk on YouTube. It's called 'Minding Your Mitochondria' and I guarantee it won't disappoint. It lasts just under eighteen minutes and sets out in layman's terms why it's so important that all of us, each and every one of us, thinks about what we put into our bodies.

In March 2016 I signed up with a personal trainer who specialises in food and nutrition. I'm no expert on the subject of food, but I also now accept that unless I take it more seriously, it's likely I'll develop further health problems down the line, the same as everyone else. Whether you're training for an Ironman or not, how you refuel is vital for your long-term health; I'm convinced of this and think that most right-minded people are in agreement. If your nutrition and fuelling strategy are correct, then the knock-on effect is mental clarity, and subsequently you'll develop an iron mindset which will help you achieve the goals you set yourself. With this in mind, please think about how you fuel your body and what you put in it.

One of my biggest frustrations in the field of endurance sports is that there's lots of conflicting information around what to eat and what not to eat. There's no doubt that money rules the world, and this is no different in endurance sports and the fitness industry – it's evident in the large brands who compete for shelf space and who condition athletes to eat their food. I bought into this for a period of time but over the last couple of years I've paid more attention to how I fuel myself before, during and after races. I've also found myself questioning the philosophies around endurance sports and nutrition, which I feel is a good thing.

Sports Gels, Energy Bars and Sweets

Running my first marathon in 2011, the only option I had was to fuel myself with gels and energy bars. Throughout my training program some of the coaches I was in touch with suggested that at mile eighteen I should have jelly babies at the ready because I'd be hitting the wall (whatever that meant). I'm not saying there's anything wrong with gels, energy bars and sweets; however, given that I've carried out my own research in this area, I now feel there are much better ways to fuel yourself during races.

So why then do so many athletes eat this stuff? Well, marketers do a fantastic job at selling the idea that these foods are exactly what you need to be eating. The PR machines are in full swing and have been since television and marketing executives realized they could actually determine what people believe and decide to eat. It's logical therefor that people fall into this way of thinking without question.

Another reason is that we're told we need to fuel our bodies every fifteen to thirty minutes to keep our energy levels up and to sustain longer training sessions. Unfortunately this leads to an over-consumption of food which results in weight gain, sluggishness and upset stomachs with cramps and sickness. If you take a closer look at these types of foods, they contain high levels of sugar among other not-so-good ingredients. After a few years of research, I know these products are not for me, and I advise you to be wary of them and the levels you consume.

For me, it's becoming increasingly clear that the optimum way to re-fuel is with real food. I appreciate this isn't the conventional way but I've never been one to follow the crowd for the sake of it. If you look into nutrition in more detail, you might see the reasons I've decided to take this path. Since being on this journey of adventure racing, and now a similar one with food and nutrition, being curious, I've studied athletes like endurance and ultimate triathlon legend Luke Tyburski – someone I'm proud to call my friend, and someone you've already heard from in the foreword of this book. Luke challenges the fuelling strategy of the bigger companies and promotes athletes eating only real food to fuel themselves during training and races. Luke's first endurance event was a double Ironman, if you don't mind, and, funnily enough, his real food sources got him to the end of it and continue to keep him strong throughout his epic adventures. In 2015

Luke completed the ultimate triathlon: swimming, cycling and running two thousand kilometres in twelve days – a challenge he designed himself. This is an incredible feat, and guess what? He fuelled himself using only real food. How inspiring. I encourage you to read his story and see his super energy levels for yourself on his website: www.luketyburski.com. Make sure you don't miss his fantastic work in the kitchen. He has loads of recipes on his website for those who aspire to take their food journey a little bit further.

If you're truly passionate about a subject in life, you'll find yourself drawn to people in that area. For me, it's finding people who've faced huge adversity in their lives, dealt with it and, more interestingly, have went on to survive and thrive. For example, I've come across an incredibly impressive and strong individual called Rich Roll whose story touched me and has inspired the endurance racing and nutritional elements of my life. Rich is a husband, devoted dad, former successful commercial lawyer and a recovering alcoholic. He is also the author of the highly acclaimed book *Finding Ultra*. I was compelled to read this book from cover to cover in a few hours as Rich's story along with his down-to-earth delivery is so powerful. Rich has an amazing story to tell, and I won't ruin it for you, but he completed five Ironman events in five days in Hawaii and, curiously enough, fuels himself with a plant-based, whole-food diet; Rich doesn't eat meat, rather he feeds himself with fruit, vegetables, grains, nuts and seeds. Like with Luke, I feel you'll be a more knowledgeable athlete, and maybe even a better person, if you get the opportunity to look at Rich's website, www.richroll.com, and read his book. In 2016 I met Rich and his beautiful wife, Julie, in Ireland, and I had the pleasure of hearing him speak. He didn't disappoint, and it was wonderful to hear some of his musings on life, adversity, food and well-being. He's certainly someone who has inspired me to develop and better myself.

Coming across Rich's work, it was certainly one of the first times I had heard of a plant-based diet and I was intrigued immediately. How could anyone survive only on a plant-based, whole-food diet? Initially I thought it was unsustainable – through ignorance mostly – as I wasn't aware of the wide range of foods to choose from; however, I knew it was something I wanted to investigate further. Without getting into it in too much detail, after months of research, in January 2016 I decided to introduce a plant-based diet into my life. Interestingly I've just experienced my longest period of wellness with the neutralisation of many of my MS symptoms. The main reason I chose this way to fuel is that it presented a compelling argument post my investigations and was, I felt, the optimum way to fuel, and also help me fight disease. Furthermore, it's incredible the number of top-end sportsmen and women who have decided to go down this nutritional route. Scott Jurek, the well-known ultra marathon tough guy, has been plant based since 1997 and is passionate about the plant-based, whole-food diet and the role it plays in endurance sports, recovery and overall health. The following athletes are all now working off a plant-based, whole-food diet:

RICH ROLL turned his life around by adopting a plant-based, whole-food diet after being unable to climb his own staircase at the age of forty due to a lifestyle of alcoholism, drugs, poor diet and negative mindset. He now travels the world telling his story of how everything improved when he decided to only put plants and whole foods on his plate. He got into exercise in a big way and was fortunate to gain an entry to Ultra man 2008 in Hawaii. In 2009 he was named one of the fittest men in the world by *Men's Fitness*. He's now an authority on food, exercise and well-being across the world and his podcast is in the top ten downloads on iTunes. Check him out, guys.

DAVID HAYE, the former two-times world champion heavy-weight boxer, is now completely powered by plants. He said, 'A lot of the meat that people eat has been genetically modified, or if it hasn't then the food the animal's been fed has been. That's tough for a human being to process, so cutting it out made me feel immediately better and stronger than ever.' Haye also believes that there are enough health grounds for him to embrace this new way to fuel. 'I used to get eczema but don't any more; used to get dandruff, now I don't. I simply feel a lot stronger since I have went plant based.'

TIM SHIEFF is a professional free runner. He runs and jumps over obstacles (as well as leaping between buildings) in an urban environment. Winner of the 2009 World Free Run Championships, Tim became vegan because of his beliefs in animal liberation. His vegan diet also provides health benefits such as a 'burst of energy and enthusiasm' in training. Previously suffering from tendonitis, Tim found that his plant-based, whole-food diet gave him stronger joints.

SERENA AND VENUS WILLIAMS are two of the most successful tennis players of all time and have recently switched to a plant-based vegan diet to fuel themselves. Their own story is very interesting to me personally as they adopted their diet after Venus discovered she had a chronic and alarming condition called Sjogren's syndrome. This forced the champion to abandon her career and it was then that she took the decision to change her eating habits. Through time and her new diet she has regained her energy and went back to tennis. Serena followed suit and both are now passionate about their new diets.

I would encourage you to look at the evidence for a whole-food, plant-based diet and form your own opinion as to what is the best food to put on your plate. I would suggest that this is more important than any adventure race you may be considering because if you're healthy enough and have optimum mental clarity, you'll achieve the majority of your goals and go on to develop that iron mindset.

As my journey with adventure racing keeps moving forward, there is now a plethora of information that I need to take on board to understand what foods to avoid and what foods to include in my diet. I'm passionate about becoming a stronger person, one with an iron mind, one who is ahead of the game, and if I'm to reach that goal, the food that I eat plays a massive part.

I'm also living with MS, and I've come to understand that what I eat from here on in may determine how healthy I'll be for the rest of my life. I truly believe this is the case, and I do appreciate that it's a big statement to make, but the more research I do the more accurate this position appears to be. I have the conviction to say this because I've taken the time to understand MS and fully research the impact and role my environment has to play in my health and my future.

Your environment is, of course, what you eat, what you drink, how you move, the air you breathe and how you think and interact with people. Are you aware that scientists today believe that the environment you keep will determine seventy to ninety-five per cent of the chance you have of developing an autoimmune disorder, obesity, heart disease or mental health problem? That's incredible, and I'm perplexed as to why I haven't been privy to this information long before now. It wasn't until I came across the good work of Dr. Terry Wahls that I was properly informed, and when I share this with others they too find it quite incredible. This type of information is so important for all of us, and I'm frustrated at times as to why it's not more widely known and discussed. For example, why has my GP never mentioned anything about how important the environment I choose to keep is to my all round well-being? What is your own doctor's advice regarding food and nutrition? I suspect you're getting little to no guidance on this matter, which in this day and age is unacceptable. The reason your GP won't go into detail about food and nutrition is because they very likely know little about it as at medical school it isn't studied in any great detail. I find this baffling given the amount of information that is out there now around food and its connection to disease.

Throughout my life I've asked questions, the uncomfortable questions that most people are afraid to ask. At school I was never scared to ask a question of the teacher no matter how silly it seemed; the same through university, and I've carried this trait into my successful business career. At thirty-eight years of age and with four Ironman events, six marathons and a handful of triathlons under my belt I now find myself asking questions about food and nutrition and looking to the discipline of medicine to see what it is and isn't saying about nutrition. The food I eat every day, the food I refuel with when I'm training – I want to know the connection between it and disease. For example, in the last twelve months I've found evidence from multiple sources linking proteins in cow's milk and dairy produce to the development of multiple sclerosis in people who are susceptible to the disease. I'm fairly pissed off that I never knew about it before now. Growing up I was only aware of the anecdotal stories that drinking milk gave you stronger bones – apparently even this information is bullshit as the calcium we get from milk comes from the plants and grass the cows eat. It seems us consumers feel the need for a middle man – in this instance the cow – which is a little absurd. If you want more information on this subject, I encourage you to look at the fascinating documentaries 'Forks Over Knives' and 'Food Choices'. Both are full of powerful information around food, and I've become a better athlete and a more-informed person since watching them and taking the facts on board.

Swim, Bike, Run

One thing I did know was that if I was going to get through the next twenty weeks, I had to plan my nutrition. I was four years in to studying the work of Dr. Wahls, had reviewed the work of Dr. Roy Swank and had also taken on board many of the recommendations set out by Dr. George Jelinek.

Dr. Roy Swank's work is well known in the world of medicine and also familiar to many in the Multiple Sclerosis community. He produced research to confirm that a diet low in saturated fat was beneficial to people who suffer from MS overall health. Many people feel that Swank's work has not got the credit is deserves over the years, and there might be a number of reasons for this namely it doesn't go down well with many within the food industry. Dr. Jelinek is someone who I have admired and followed for years and would put him down as someone who inspired me greatly to take control of my own wellbeing. He is an Australian neurologist who lives very well with Multiple Sclerosis and is the guy who is responsible for creating the Overcoming MS program that is now followed by thousands of people across the world. All three of these medical professionals have committed their entire life's work to find out what people can do to fight/prevent disease and achieve their potential. It's just a pity most of us only stumble upon people like this whenever we have been diagnosed with a medical problem. Well that's another story altogether and maybe something I will cover in my next book.

In any case there is now an abundance of information which will help you decide what you should be putting into your body. I'm certainly no authority, but I suggest that you do your own research and you'll arrive upon the right path for you. If you're feeling overwhelmed by all the conflicting information out there, I encourage you to seek the help of an expert who can navigate you round the field.

There were two areas of my food plan that I needed to focus on: the first being a plan that would keep me strong Monday to Sunday and the second being that it provided me with enough energy to keep me fuelled to complete the training program and the six events of my challenge. At this stage I had already started to move towards a vegan diet, so for my weekly plan I aimed for a hunter-gatherer diet somewhere between The Wahls Protocol, the Paleo diet and my own food plan; I would eat as much fruit and vegetables as I possibly could and combine this with fish. Over the years, and I'm not too sure why this happened, I've went off animal meat. I was never a big steak eater anyway. Chicken, if anything, would have been my preference, but after my research my instincts swayed me off meat for the most part. I believe that fish is healthier and is the best option for me, but I'm not encouraging you to follow my approach to food, I'm merely sharing my preferences and personal experiences.

With my meal plans sorted for during the week, I then thought about the best way to refuel during training and races. I had six events, some of them quite long, so time was of the essence if I was to give my body a period to get accustomed to a new way of eating with minimum disruption to my gut. I never really bought into the whole gel-carbohydrate-thing, and truthfully I was looking for something healthy to fuel me, so I had a chat with Luke and he suggested I look at a new company, 33Shake. When I read their opening line on their website, I was sold:

We are 33Shake and we make the finest sports nutrition on the planet. 100% natural, you have never seen anything like this before.

My plan was in place: to fuel myself with natural food which would provide me with the sustenance I needed to get me through the next twenty weeks of endurance events and achieve my goal of becoming an Ironman. I didn't waste any time in checking out my 33Shake products and immediately incorporated them into my training. It was clear from the start that these shakes and gels were great for my energy levels, were easily carried on the run and the bike and, more importantly, didn't upset my stomach. Perfect.

Food on a Typical Day

There's no doubt that the nutritional part of this journey is much easier if you're interested in food and cooking. I've been cooking for myself since I was eighteen and I really enjoy preparing and eating food. It's even better now as I'm getting my children to eat a healthier diet, so we're all enjoying the ride. Here's what a typical day's eating might look like for me:

- A large bowl of organic porridge with fruit, normally blueberries and pears, flaxseed, hemp and protein powder thrown in for good measure.
- I snack during the day on almonds and cashews with fruit, usually blueberries, raspberries, bananas and apples.
- I drink between two and three litres of water every day.

- I have salad at lunch and my dinner is a large plate of healthy food. The regulars include lots of cooked vegetables in coconut oil, basmati rice and sweet potato – all great sources of protein.
- I drink a few cups of coffee a day, but only up to three in the afternoon, and in the evening I drink green or peppermint tea along with water.

Food for Racing and Training

- I start with a bowl of organic porridge and snack on some nuts and fruit.
- I sip water throughout the day and also have electrolytes in my drink during races.
- I use 33Shake to fuel me throughout races and training with bananas and nuts when I need more energy.
- I now avoid gels and energy bars where possible, as I find they are not great for your gut.

As I said, it takes time to work out your optimum food plan, so make sure you experiment and find the right refueling strategy for you.

The Walled City Marathon

I was thirteen weeks into my thirty-week training program and things were generally going well. I have come to understand running a household, a business and training for an Ironman that time is my most valuable asset, one I can't waste; every minute, hour and day is a prisoner. The only way for me to live now (this is as a result of the program and a blessing in my eyes) is as a structured and disciplined person always working to a plan. This was hard to implement and familiarise myself with, but thirteen weeks in I was enjoying the new adventure and the structure it brought to my life.

Event number two was coming up, The Walled City Marathon. On reflection I didn't know how the hell I had got round Belfast City Marathon a few weeks previous because of my lack of training the month before. The last few miles of that race were horrendous, and I was just hoping that because I was able to train right up to this marathon, I would be better prepared and in much better physical shape for this one.

A marathon is a tremendous challenge in its own right, a tough challenge, a very personal one; however, if you do the work and apply yourself, it can be a life-changing experience. It certainly was for me back in 2011 and for anyone else I've ever spoken to about it, and that's why I'd encourage you to think seriously about taking up the challenge.

The Walled City Marathon was only in its second year with fantastic feedback which meant I was really looking forward to the race. Preparation is key so I thought it important to travel up to Derry the night before and stay in a hotel, chill out and relax before the race. It worked out well as the hotel upgraded me to a huge room – perfect. I had a beautiful meal of steamed cod on a bed of vegetables washed down with a litre or so of water. Hard to beat, I hear you say, and so it was. I find it hard to sleep the night before an endurance race as my mind does somersaults and can't switch off. That night was no different and I tossed and turned in the bed thinking about how the race would pan out for me the following morning.

The good news was I was running with my old sparring partner Gmac again, so I was looking forward to taking in everything Derry had to throw at me. My race plan was to take it easy over the first eighteen miles, suck up the atmosphere and see how Gmac was getting on. I'd take it handy over the next six miles and at mile twenty-four leave Gmac for dead and cruise home. I nailed the plan to a T, but Gmac didn't find it funny as he's a competitive devil himself. I don't think he could get over how explosive I was after twenty-four miles, and it was great to see his face at the finishing line. To be fair to him he's a great sport and for the age of him ran a steady race himself.

What stands out for me in this marathon was mile twenty-three when we turned Free Derry Corner and made our way up the steep hill into the city centre. This marathon was the marathon of four seasons – as I called it in a subsequent blog post – as we had all seasons of weather throughout the race. Coming up the hill, the hailstones crashing down on us like meteorites and the wind and rain making conditions brutal, my form was absolutely rubbish. However, like all marathons, no matter where you are in the world, the supporters who come out whatever the weather are the heart and soul of the event. As I reached the summit of the hill I noticed a young lady's handwritten, presumably motivational, quote on a piece of cardboard held out towards us runners. This was no Henry Ford, Jim Rohn or Tony Robbins quote, no. It was typical Derry sense of humour and very sympathetic for all the runners coming up to twenty-four miles at the top of a sharply inclined hill. It simply read 'Wiser Eating Grass'. I was in a fair amount of pain at this stage, but over the next couple of miles I didn't think of anything else and it spurred me home and across the line with a huge smile on my face. That's what marathons are all about: pain, endurance, grit, hope, humour and downright doggedness to get your body over the finishing line. The confidence I felt in completing the marathon was tremendous – it was my second marathon in a month, event number two in the bag, and I was delighted with my effort. Another medal and, more importantly, no injuries so my plan for September was on track. I wasn't as tired after this marathon and I was convinced this was a direct result of my training regime. My energy levels were good and it was clear my refueling plan was coming together. My training over the last thirteen weeks, including my bad days, was delivering physically and, more importantly, mentally. It was now seven months or so since Christmas and with two challenges down and only four to go I was making super progress. I was certainly out of my comfort zone and growing as a person and an athlete. The endorphins released from the first two challenges were very empowering. I believed that my dream was possible, that my dream was becoming a reality.

CHAPTER 6

Fall down seven times, get up eight.
CHINESE PROVERB

Perseverance

As I've strived to overcome illness, meet adventures head-on, run a successful business, achieve my goals and look after my family, inspirational quotes have become an important part of my artillery in developing an iron mindset to deal with the turbulence and clutter we are all too familiar with in this day and age. Between reading, social networking and coming up with my own thoughts and ideas and reciting these in my head, I read over one hundred quotes every day. It's now an essential part of my daily routine and genuinely helps me overcome the challenges that come my way. I was very aware that there were going to be lots of times when I would want to give up during my training program and Ironman journey. I was particularly concerned about the swim and the bike as I was quite weak at both sports; however, I knew the only way to turn this around was to make sure I clocked up enough training hours.

Perseverance: persistence in doing something despite difficulty or delay in achieving success. (*Oxford English Dictionary*)

This is a fantastic quality to have in your locker. The thing about perseverance is that even if you don't have a lot of it in you right now, I have found it is something you can acquire and build up, if you follow the right plan and approach everything with the right attitude. There are a number of ways to do this, and I'm going to share three with you now:

Surround yourself with good people – this is not just essential to help you develop and increase your levels of perseverance, surrounding yourself with good people is needed for you to get along in life and make progress. Over the last few years I've met people who've become influential in my own life and development. These people probably don't even know who they are, but they continue to shape me and push me on. If you're goal-oriented in any way, it's important that you sound out those people who are successful and have achieved things in their lives that you are trying to achieve. If you can surround yourself with people like this, then the beautiful thing is that you can tap into their mindset.

Find an inspiration – I talk about inspiration when I speak in schools and universities, with business owners and groups of people. It's very important in life that you find an inspiration, someone or something you admire. It's people like this who will subsequently inspire you to achieve your dreams and goals in life. Inspirational people are everywhere. In my case, my family inspire me – each and every one of them. My mum and dad worked hard for many years to support me and my siblings, they were there for us all the way and are still the backbone of my support unit – two incredibly strong and resilient people. My sister is a strong woman bringing up a big family; an incredible mum running her own business with her husband. My youngest brother, Barry, left Ireland for Australia many years ago to start a new life. He works hard, is doing well and now has a family of his own. My brother Colm is a few years younger than me, and is one hell of a strong man. He's always on the end of the phone offering help in any way. Inspirational people are everywhere, so you have no excuse not to sound them out and watch as they inspire you to complete your challenge, be successful in business and face down adversity.

When I was really ill with MS in 2009, I went to the gym a few times a week. There was a guy there who'd been in a very serious car accident which had damaged his spinal cord and subsequently he could hardly walk and was in a lot of pain every day. I noticed that he never missed a session, never gave up, and three times a week he was in the gym, working hard and trying to get strong. He never knew this but that guy inspired me every single day to keep fighting against MS and to never give up. My only regret is I never actually told him so, which, in hindsight, I should have done.

In the last few years I've made a point of finding people who've overcome challenges and faced adversity down. When I find someone new it's exciting for me, as I know I can tap into a new mindset and in the process acquire new skills. Each of them will have perseverance in abundance, and when you study them their drive and determination becomes contagious. So get with the program and identify those people in your family circle, your community, your country and across the world who inspire you.

Improve your attitude – a bad attitude is like a flat tyre: you won't get very far. I've met many successful people, high achievers, top sportsmen and women and great community people, and one trait they all have in common is that they've developed a good attitude.

In my book, *Attitude Is Everything*, the profound message I wanted to get across was that despite setbacks and challenges if you approach these with the right attitude, absolutely anything is possible. To obtain the levels of perseverance I would need to get to the Ironman finish line, I knew I had to improve my attitude. I had set myself a huge challenge with my Against All Odds campaign, and there was no way I was going to get through it if I didn't have the right approach and attitude. This is a fundamental requirement to life, and it's something I'll have to continue to work on for many years.

One thing though, if you surround yourself with good people and gravitate towards inspirational people and situations, the hybrid of this will be an improvement and strengthening of your attitude and your mind. There is nothing easy in life, and the only way to get to where you want to go is to stick with your plan and apply a consistent, accountable approach to the delivery of your primary goals.

Week Fifteen

I was halfway through my training program. My midterm report probably would read something like this:

- Doing well
- Attitude spot on
- Needs to work harder in training
- Needs to improve nutrition and look at weekly calorie intake
- Needs to sleep more and make more use of foam roller (a horrible piece of kit)

Overall this was quite good, and considering I had two marathons in the bag, my strength and confidence levels had risen immensely since the start of my campaign. This was very real, and I only had another fifteen weeks to prepare for one of the toughest events known to man. What I'd noticed in the last few weeks was that I was definitely getting stronger and my fear of the Ironman was subsiding. This was a positive development as I'd been quite anxious about it previously, a feeling I'd kept to myself. A lot of things had been causing me anxiety over the last couple of months, and feeling my stress levels subside was a welcome development.

My next event was in two weeks and I was really excited about it: the Derry Sprint Triathlon. It was my third consecutive year taking part, so I knew what to expect. Sprint triathlons are great, and Derry in particular excels itself with bigger crowds and more athletes year-on-year. I was glad to be over my two marathons and was looking forward to improving my technique in the water and on the bike for Derry. My training program was going well, and on my rest day, Monday, I usually had a massage to help my body recover. Rest is one area that any newbie athlete training for an event needs to research. The human body can only do so much, and it's when you're sleeping and resting that the body actually gets a chance to repair itself and grow stronger. If you don't rest enough, it puts too much stress on your muscles and joints. With my intense program I was keen to avoid this, so rest, massage and recovery were three key ingredients in my plan.

On the Road Again

The appeal of triathlons for me is that there's lots to organise; my brain has to be activated and engaged for this sport, so for the Derry Sprint Triathlon I packed the car the night before because I knew it would take me ninety minutes or so getting the length of the city in the morning. My bike was in the boot and my box of gear – wetsuit, helmet, cycling shoes, Vaseline and goggles among other requirements – was in the back seat. I also had my bag of goodies to give me energy to get me round the course.

At 8.30 a.m. the starter's gun went off and over five hundred triathletes made their way into the River Foyle to start the 2015 Derry Sprint Triathlon. I lowered myself into the water very slowly because it was absolutely freezing despite it being the start of summer – remember, this is Northern Ireland.

I took a few strokes, relaxed and thought only good thoughts, or that was the plan anyway. Not so long ago water petrified me thanks to the Jaws' films, and although I was fairly certain there were no man-eating sharks in the River Foyle that morning, the thought of some monster lifting me out of the water and tossing me upside down continued to trickle through my neurological pathways. Why the hell does that happen?

The swim went very well, which was extremely satisfying. My plan to relax in the water, find a spot with plenty of room where nobody would elbow me in the mouth and focus on my rhythm worked a treat. I got out of the water alive – always a plus – and headed to transition, quickly changed and jumped onto the dream machine to tackle the hilly bike course. The crowds played their part and I sailed out of transition to rapturous applause; I don't think it was directed at me in particular but sure, for the craic, let's believe it was. The bike course was two laps of the city with a couple of nasty hills thrown in for good measure. I was riding my Felt triathlon bike, an amazing piece of equipment. Having never liked cycling, I now find it quite enjoyable given that I can get up to twenty-five miles per hour on the straight. The bike is always fast in Derry, and in the sprint distance there's no other way to ride than to give it your all, which is what I did. I arrived back into transition feeling strong with my plan for the run to start steady, lift the pace after the first half mile and put one foot in front of the other to the finishing line.

The correct equipment to help you get round a triathlon course is vital, and that includes the running shoes. I've experimented with a number of brands but this season I've settled on Hoka. A tremendous shoe that gives me all the support and confidence I need and that makes running more enjoyable. Regardless of what was on my feet, it's always a beautiful run in Derry over the Peace Bridge and through the scenic park route. After an hour and thirty-two minutes yours truly crossed the line at the end of a strong run. It was a great event and I was feeling really strong and all the better for taking part in the race. Event number three was in the bag and there was only another twelve weeks to Ironman. Time was moving on quickly. The good thing about the Derry triathlon is that I was through it injury free, a major bonus. I knew it was a challenge to stay in one piece, my body intact, for six events, which was why I paid due attention to my rest and recovery days and my food plan. That was the key, and so far it was working.

Structure

It was now the beginning of July, and I was into week nineteen of my training program with three events done and dusted. This week the training hours increased to twelve and a half with the toughest session being a sixty-mile cycle on Saturday. It's absolutely crucial if you're considering an event like Ironman to have a training program. There are hundreds on the Internet and lots of information on how to prepare for endurance sports, so make sure you find the one that works for you. Don Fink's plan was working very well for me, and what I liked about it was it fitted in perfectly with my work and family life. Mostly I was doing some form of training for an hour Tuesday to Friday with the longer rides and runs at the weekend.

On Saturday, 4 July, I set out at stupid o'clock to get in my long cycle. There's no doubt that the bike is the hardest part of all this for me; I get bored, so I listen to podcasts to help me get through the longer sessions. That ride took me three hours and forty minutes to complete and it wasn't that bad after all. I had some podcasts on the wire and I got my fuel right, so my overall mood was quite good. It's shit getting up so early at the week-end to do a long cycle on your own, but I slipped in the back door at ten and Lilyanna and Conor Junior never even knew I was away. I finished week nineteen with a ninety-minute run on Sunday mixing it up with some hill sprints for good measure. Another week gone and I was feeling a lot stronger for it. The hard work of the past few months was paying off. Physically my body was finding a new shape which I loved and mentally I was in the zone. I had to stay there for another while yet as there was plenty more hard work ahead.

I had three weeks to my next event which would be the fourth in my twenty weeks challenge. The Belfast Olympic Triathlon was another race I was familiar with and looking forward to. My training program was still working really well, which I was delighted with, but unfortunately I'd picked up a small problem with my groin. I wasn't sure exactly how it had happened, but it was hurting me more mentally than physically. There wasn't any significant damage, I was sure of that, but I decided that I wouldn't do any running or cycling for a while to give it time to rest and recover. The great thing about triathlon is that if you're carrying a knock like this, you can still get in the pool, which suited me as I was a poor swimmer and needed to practice as much as possible. For the next two weeks I clocked up extra hours in the water, and just as the experts tell you, the more work you put into anything the better return you get. My swimming was coming on well, to the point that I was able to lift my head and breathe to the left and right while swimming. I was certainly no expert by any stretch, but I knew that to swim over 2.4 miles in the sea with three thousand other people I needed to sight left and right – primarily for safety, never mind technique. I found it helpful to watch YouTube videos of people learning to swim too. I watched quite a few and it's amazing the pointers you pick up from a few short videos. For the first time I was settled in the water and improving my technique. If I could keep this up, I would be ready for the big one.

My groin problem was easing, which was good news, but I was managing another problem: intermittent MS symptoms. For the previous week or so, my hands and face had pins and needles and my energy levels were quite low. I've learned to live with this shit now as I've dealt with it for nine years, but it still gets me down at times. I didn't need a full-on relapse of my MS now – that would more or less rule my Ironman dream out. Normally what happens is that I feel quite rough for a few days and then it settles, and thankfully that's what happened this time. A good job too because my next event was in a few days and I needed to be ready.

Belfast Olympic Triathlon

The night before event four the heavens opened in majestic fashion with the forecast of high winds and torrential rain for the next morning. It was the end of July and supposedly mid-summer but we're accustomed to unpredictable, shit weather in this part of the world. My alarm went off at half six, and I peeked behind the curtains hoping to see the sun coming up. As it was I nearly lost my nose through the slightly open window when a great burst of wind tried to suck me out – lovely. The rain was dancing off the glass like Michael Flatley on Red Bull and the trees were blowing side to side as if two jumbo jets were about to take off immediately in front of them. It was a horrendous morning weather-wise, and as the thought of climbing back under the duvet started to overcome me, I went into autopilot and headed down to the kitchen to prepare breakfast.

Following several rounds of toast and porridge with honey, I jumped into the car, which thankfully I'd had the good sense to pack the night before, and headed for Belfast. I parked as close to transition as I could, got my gear out of the car and readied myself for the race. Despite the crap weather the triathletes appeared to be in good enough sprits, and as the course director battled with the elements to read out the rules and regulations, the now standard triathlon buzz set in – even though I could hardly feel my toes.

I was in wave two of the swim, so I didn't have long to hang around before the horn blared, and, as usual, I looked for a spot in the water where nobody else could annoy me. Slowly but surely I relaxed into my swim and headed north up the River Lagan with over seven hundred other competitors. I was swimming a distance of just under a mile, and as the rain danced off the water I kept my thoughts positive and focused on one stroke after another. More than once I questioned my sanity and the rationale of swimming towards Scotland in freezing water with the wind and rain blowing and a stack of other insane people at eight thirty on a Sunday morning. However, I survived those dark moments alright, and in what felt like no time at all I had completed another good swim. I pulled myself out of the water and walked – yes, walked – to transition where I made the change into my bike gear and started what would be a challenging enough bike course in this horrible weather. The wind was up and over the next hour the intensity of the rain increased dramatically making the course both dangerous and unpleasant. The only real positive was that I avoided a puncture but there appeared to be many unfortunate athletes in that position, given the number changing their tyres at the roadside. I was struggling mentally, and was fighting with myself to stay positive and focused and just to keep going. These were easily the worst weather conditions I'd experienced in my triathlon career, and it was really pissing me off. I'm struggling to think of many more depressing moments in life than finding yourself cycling against a gale-force wind in the pissing rain – I challenge you to come up with a few.

Ever the trooper and an Ironman in the making, I wasn't for throwing the towel in just yet. I hung in there and after what felt like an eternity I had only one kilometre left to complete a shit bike course. In transition I spent ten minutes trying to thaw out my numb toes and struggled to get into my shoes. I detest the cold, it exacerbates my MS symptoms and makes everything feel so shit; if you add the wind and rain, well, you've guessed how I felt. The elements were turning this race into one of my toughest yet, and, I suppose if I could get through this, it would be another step in my development of a mindset fit for Majorca. Finally I got my trainers on and set off on the run. As usual, I settled after the first mile and got into my stride. I crossed the finishing line in some two hours and fifty-eight minutes; given the weather I was delighted as there were times, during the bike in particular, that I felt extremely tested mentally. Thankfully my groin didn't play me up too badly because an injury on top of the weather might have been all a bit much. The weather made this event one of the hardest I've competed in, which made it all the sweeter to get another Olympic triathlon under my belt and another medal for my 'great wall' at home. I'd now completed four events in fifteen-odd weeks, and after I'd collected my medal I thawed out in the car and reflected on my achievements.

In 2007 my neurologist told me I wouldn't play football again, that my life would be more difficult and would change forever. Elements of that are true, fair enough; however, in my opinion I was being conditioned to believe that I would be very sick and not able to do things that others could. One of the nicest things about my recovery is continuing to throw the so-called rule book in the bin – an empowering feeling. I say all the time: do not accept what people tell you as gospel; ask questions, research, interrupt, challenge the status quo, because if you do and you continue to seek answers to important questions, it will lead to you developing an iron mind and a winning mindset.

The last few weeks had been tough, intense, and the Olympic triathlon was a proper challenge; however, I continued to get stronger and was now ready and looking forward to my half Ironman in Dublin in two weeks. For the first time in a few months everything was starting to come together.

CHAPTER 7

> The first step is, you have to say that you can.
>
> UNKNOWN

I Can and I Will

In just over a week I'd be competing in my first official Ironman event: Dublin's 70.3. It was week twenty-four of Don Fink's training plan and so far I had completed two marathons, one sprint triathlon and one Olympic triathlon, and thankfully I was still in one piece. My Just Giving page had raised over £3200 for charity and my story was getting some traction with the media, which was fantastic. I was well and truly riding the wave at this point with my business going through a period of sustained growth, so every second was a prisoner as I was super busy. At times I found my lunchtime training slots quite tight to fit in, but thankfully I was still able to keep up the program which was extremely important and crucial to my overall success. I was reading like crazy and bought another couple of Ironman books which were giving me a greater understanding of what it would take to get round the course in one piece. I had added visualisation into my program, something many of the world's leading sportsmen and women practice regularly to develop that winning mentality. I consistently visualised myself in the race in Majorca, and, more importantly, finishing it. Visualisation is a topic I'll get into later, but suffice to say I've been practicing it since I read

Napoleon Hill's classic *Think and Grow Rich* a few years ago. Visualisation really helps me get my head round challenges and deal with situations powerful enough to knock me off course. If used correctly, I believe visualisation can play a very positive role in giving you an extra few percent when your back's against the wall.

Monday, 3 August 2015

I set the alarm for six o'clock and after what felt like a few minutes' sleep it beeped like crazy. I'd best get up and at it. I prepared breakfast before the rest of the house woke. I've found the morning to be the most peaceful and productive time of the day for me as it allows me to focus, get a good meal into my body and plan the day ahead. A friend taught me a series of Chinese exercises called Chi Gung, an exercise that lets you enter a state of calm which works by relaxing the body and mind. If you're open-minded, I recommend you take a class or check it out on YouTube. I've found it to be very beneficial and that morning I did a good fifteen-minute session before the children got up and kicked-off the madness. Today was rest day – the day I enjoyed the most. I had a light pool session in the diary with a sauna and steam room penciled in afterwards. I was looking forward to taking things easier today and letting my body recover because I had a run, a bike, a swim and a strength session in the diary before I headed to Dublin on Saturday to register for Sunday's event. This was an exciting week, and Sunday was going to be an important day because it was a huge step up in distance compared to what I was used to. I spent a couple of hours reading through the rules and regulations for Sunday's event. It was a little head wrecking because due to the increased distance in the race the transitions were miles apart, and it took me a while to get my head around how it was all going to work. But with a few triathlons now well and truly under my belt, I've found that triathletes have a can-do attitude in abundance and just get on with whatever's thrown at them. It's all part of the journey of finding out how triathlons actually work and how you must apply yourself to the sport if you want to make any progress with it.

I noted transition one was in Dún Laoghaire, approximately fifteen miles away from transition two in Phoenix Park which is close to Dublin city centre, so I made my way into Dún Laoghaire on Saturday afternoon to drop my bike off, and it was clear to see that the Ironman roadshow had arrived: large trailers were parked up at the beachfront, vast crowds were everywhere and music was pumping out the sound systems. This was my first proper experience of how Ironman puts on a show, and, I have to tell you, my adrenaline was flowing and I liked what I saw. I ventured into transition and my excitement got the better of me. Anyone who's ever been to Dún Laoghaire will agree that the setting on the beachfront with the horizon as the backdrop is incredible. Ironman had clearly done its homework and had chosen the perfect setting for tomorrow's race.

I needed to go to transition two in Phoenix Park to register by four o'clock, so I had to get my skates on. I struggled to find a parking space at Phoenix Park because of the hundreds of cars and crowds of people, but being full of enthusiasm it wasn't annoying me too much. Eventually I got sorted and made my way to registration. I collected my pack from the big tent in the middle of Phoenix Park and had a quick peek at my goody bag. There was a great buzz around base camp, smiling faces, athletes and their families all in super form including me who was buzzing that I'd come so far in the short space of five months. Tomorrow I was competing in a half Ironman – something I couldn't have dreamed possible a few years ago when I was diagnosed with multiple sclerosis and more or less told my life was over.

I reminded myself how hard I'd worked to get to Dublin in peak physical condition, and that if I got through tomorrow injury free, Majorca was mine for the taking. I'd stuck with my plan, I'd been disciplined with my food, so I had great confidence for tomorrow's race. Anyone who knows triathlon knows it's important to get a good meal and proper rest the night before a race, and as I'd spent enough time looking around Phoenix Park, I started to make my way back to my hotel and hit the hay. An early night for CD.

Race Day 70.3

At five thirty I pulled myself out of bed. I hadn't had the best night's sleep but thankfully I'd been in bed early enough to get a good few hours. It was still dark outside but I got my stuff together pronto to drive the short distance to the bus that would take me to Dún Laoghaire. I fuelled up with a swift bowl of porridge and some fruit followed by a couple of glasses of orange juice and a few nuts before the obligatory cup of coffee. Happily, I'd prepared my breakfast the night before, so I was off to a good start because time was at a premium all day. I boarded one of tens of buses with the other triathletes. Unsurprisingly, there wasn't much chat on the bus, it being stupid o'clock, but there was a slightly annoying Spanish couple who were all over each other, taking selfies and whispering sweet nothings in one another's ears – just a tad early for that carry on, I thought. We arrived in Dún Laoghaire just after seven, and the good news was that my bike was still there, safe and sound. It's very important to arrive in good time at transition on the morning of the race to make whatever adjustments are needed and final preparations are required before the starter's gun blasts off.

I reminded myself again that just over eighteen months ago I could barely swim, but with lessons, a plan, perseverance and a will to win I was competing in a half Ironman, which had a 1.2 mile sea swim. This was pretty incredible stuff and I was excited and slightly apprehensive because all my physical and mental preparation in the last few months was going to be tested in the water in the next hour or so. It was a bit overwhelming as there are no hiding places on race day.

Finally the shot rang out and all the triathletes, some two and a half thousand of us, began the staggered start to the race. As always, I walked into the water quite slowly. I took my time and sucked it all up concentrating on my breathing technique and trying to relax, my strategy being to position myself at the left-hand side of the field, and, slow as you like, off I went. It was an amazing sight to behold – such a stunning morning with the sun rising from the west – and as I dipped in and out of the water I could hear the buzzing of the Ironman drone filming above us. The start was surprisingly good for me, and after about ten minutes I got into my rhythm. It was such a great feeling racing in the water. This was a big step up from the other triathlons I'd completed in the last two years, but it was easily the best buzz I'd experienced in the sport. As we left the bay I was coping well with the swim, taking my time, breathing correctly and focusing on my technique. The same technique I'd spent many hours in the pool trying to perfect even though I knew that swimming in a wetsuit in open water was a completely different experience – one, I have to say, I was starting to enjoy. I felt very accomplished having got the hang of open-water swimming, a feeling that had a positive impact on my mindset. After fifty-odd minutes, which went in quite quickly, I noticed I was a mere few hundred yards from the finishing line of the swim. I couldn't believe how well I coped with the first part of the race, which gave me great confidence in my ability to finish the day strong.

As I pulled myself out of the water, the roar of the crowd was deafening with everyone in tremendous spirits. I nearly forgot I was racing and instead sucked up the atmosphere before reality hit home and I broke into a light jog to transition one to get ready for the bike course: The bike would comprise fifty-six miles in and out of Dublin before returning to the city centre for a half-marathon comprising four laps of the iconic Phoenix Park. After about ten minutes in transition – mostly fighting with my wetsuit – I was ready to go. I made the short dash to my dream machine, wheeled it over to the exit, mounted and cycled my way through Dún Laoghaire with all the other athletes.

It was impossible not to notice how well-organised the event was: it ran smoothly and the security, safety, volunteers and professionals were all in place to ensure a good event. The difference between the triathlons

I'd experienced and how Ironman went about their business was visible – pretty awesome was the only way to describe it.

I made good progress on the bike, and after thirty minutes or so I refueled my body to prepare for the long day ahead. The bike's the part of the race to get tanked up with energy but it's not uncommon for triathletes to get sucked too far into the experience and completely forget about food altogether. If this happens, you'll struggle to get through the run and possibly not finish the race at all, which would be a disaster. I reckoned the whole event would take me over six hours, so I planned to eat something every half hour. I had some 33Shake gels which I'd made up at breakfast and I also had some bars cut up for when I needed them. I'm a big fan of electrolytes, so I had these in a tube on my vest ready to go into my water to keep me hydrated. I'd done enough research in the last few months to ascertain that if I was serious about finishing the longer races strong, I needed to nail my nutrition. If I ate enough on the bike, then I'd have plenty of fuel to get me through the run. Even though I was going well at this point, it was my first time competing in longer distances, so I was fairly apprehensive as I ventured into unknown territory.

The bike is always the hardest part of a triathlon for me, and it's certainly the sport I need to put more time into. I'd struggled in training to really get into the bike, but doing an Ironman meant I needed to get my head round it quickly – my rationale being it's the part of the race I spend the most time on, so the more efficient I'm on the bike, the better I'll be at the sport.

Thankfully, after three hours on the bike, I was making my way towards transition two, all in one piece, which left me with the half-marathon to finish the course. I felt strong enough and was surprised the bike hadn't taken as much out of me as I was thought it would. Transition two it was, and time to get some fuel into me, pull the Hoka's on and make a start on the run. The atmosphere in Phoenix Park, as earlier, was electric, and it was estimated that there were some ten thousand spectators present to cheer on the athletes and get us over the line. Everywhere you looked there was a sea of colour and noise which added to the atmosphere. Running is my strongest part of triathlon, and as I completed the first-half of the run I thought about how fortunate I was taking part in such an inspiring and historic occasion, Ironman's first event in Ireland. I was some five hours into the race and knew it was important to be as positive as possible, so I focused on filling my head full of good thoughts while blocking out any pain or negative connotations. My legs were a little tired but the endorphins fizzing round my brain blocked out a lot of the tiredness and negativity. As I got closer to the line I promised to focus on finishing the race, having good thoughts and putting one foot in front of the other. My body had worked damn hard throughout the race, had held up well and I was feeling strong. I finished my first 70.3 Ironman race in six hours and twenty minutes, an incredible feeling – this was real. I'd travelled over seventy miles in water, on a bike and on foot today. All of the hard work, the dream I'd had at Christmas, all the questions I'd asked of myself had been well and truly answered today. I was on top of the world and I'd kept my multiple sclerosis at bay through the majority of it. Even if I couldn't complete the full Ironman next month, this alone would send out a very powerful message to anyone facing any kind of adversity in the world. The whole experience of the day was overwhelming and empowering. The other great thing was the medal – an absolute beast of a thing. Ironman definitely know how to put on a show and the medals are certainly worthy of the challenge they set you. I knew it would sit very well on my great wall at home.

I made my way back home to my family to fill them in on my experience. I turned the music up, sat back and just relaxed in a really good place mentally. I spent the car journey reflecting and being thankful for everything I'd achieved over the past number of months. I can be quite hard on myself and anyone training for an Ironman will tell you it's a very lonely, long and difficult road. There's nothing glamorous about getting up to train every day and putting in a lot of weekend hours away from your family while you work on your body and your mindset, but what I've found in life is that to achieve anything worthwhile, you must make sacrifices to get ahead, and this Ironman challenge was certainly one challenge where a lot of sacrifices had to be made. To temper that, what I was also finding was that the health benefits and numerous pluses that come out of a challenge like this are immeasurable and worth all the effort and pain that comes with it. In just over five weeks I'd be at the start line in Majorca, surrounded by my family, in the sun, hopefully fit and healthy and ready to take on one of the toughest adventure races in the world. On reflection, it was an incredible day, and as I got closer to home the thought of sinking into my double bed was absolutely sensational.

Thrilled to finish Barcelona 70.3 mile IM race

Belfast Olympic Triathlon

Team photo at my celebration dinner

5.30am, on the beach in Alcudia at the start of my 2.4 mile swim

My mum attending one of my talks. I get my strength from this lady.

Luke Tyburski - The Ultimate Triathlete

My younger brother Colm part of my support crew in Majorca

Lilyanna is delighted I've finished Ironman alive after 15:05 hrs

Team photo day after Ironman in Majorca – who's tired?

CHAPTER 8

I'm not telling you it's going to be easy, I'm
telling you it's going to be worth it
Anonymous

Ironman

Between 2007 and 2010, living with MS for the first few years, I was conditioned to believe – by almost everyone – that I was goosed, that I wouldn't
lead the productive, adventurous life I'd always hoped for. For close to four
years I accepted this psychology and it nearly killed me. When I talk to others now, sharing my experiences around one of the darkest moments in
my life, I often present this as time wasted. It was four years of my life that I
gave up and closed my mind off to the possibility of recovering. I wasn't interested in improving and was in a very dark and dangerous place. In 2010,
I remember sitting in a meeting with other MS patients including a lady
in a wheelchair who had been living with MS for over twenty-five years.
When I shared my story of giving up for four years, she interjected and said
she'd done the same thing, only her period of giving up lasted over nineteen
years. Nineteen years – I couldn't believe it. Such a long time to be suffering
those negative thoughts and absolute lack of hope. Thankfully one day she
found the courage to fight back against the MS, to get her mind, body and
life back, and that's exactly what she did. It took that lady nineteen years to

open her mind to the possibility that her life could improve, and guess what? That's what bloody well happened! This is powerful, and it's something that has stuck with me, and whenever I'm struggling with my thoughts it helps me channel them back onto a more positive frame of mind.

Most people in the world know Muhammad Ali as the guy who said he was the greatest boxer to ever walk on two legs. Although he may have been in the top three greatest boxers of all time, not everyone would agree with him on his assertion that he was the best. Question, do you think he actually cares what others think of him? I suspect not. His iron mindset put him apart from the other boxers of his time and set the foundations for him to achieve great things in his life and career. Like Mohammad Ali, I had to get myself into a situation whereby I believed that I could not only beat MS but also reverse the symptoms. All the literature I read at the time and all the medical experts told me this was impossible; however, as I found other people in the world who believed they could overcome their own MS – and were more importantly making progress – a fire lit in my soul. This fire has smoked and, although during the bad times it's nearly went out, I've continued to feed it with positive thoughts and ideas of beating MS and reaching my full potential.

I was very emotional when I crossed the finishing line in Dublin. I was on my own and had just completed a half Ironman, an incredible feat in its own right. It was a game changer for me and gave me so much confidence in what I could potentially achieve in my life. I had plenty of opportunity to throw the towel in over the course of the last six months, but guess what? I kept going because I've worked to develop a mindset that would not only get me through the rest of my life, but that would allow me to thrive for the rest of my life. One that was going to get me through this difficult illness, allow me to build a successful business and, most importantly, be a brilliant father to my children by making sure they had everything they needed in life. Just like Mohammad Ali, I was starting to believe I could do anything I put my mind to – and that included an Ironman.

Week 28

Two weeks to go and I was really looking forward to Majorca. It was Monday, 7 September – my allocated rest day and my favourite day of the week. I had ten hours of training in the diary for the week to come with a four-hour bike on Saturday and a two-hour run on Sunday. Things were ticking over nicely, and one of the most satisfying outcomes of the training was that, finally, I had become quite competent in the pool. I wasn't Olympic-Games standard, but I found that once I got the hang of the basic swimming technique and swam regularly, it was only possible to improve, which is exactly what happened.

The week went in as quickly as expected and Friday morning was there before I knew it. I lifted my head off the pillow and I knew I felt rough. I got up and had a quick shower, but eating my breakfast my head had that heavy, fuzzy, fucking MS-type sensation again. I really didn't need this shit to be happening right now, I seriously didn't. I knew immediately it was my MS symptoms kicking into gear, and with two weeks to go to race day, I didn't need to be dealing with this crap again. The remainder of the day was a disaster for the most part. I went into work, ever the trooper. Anyone who works for themselves will know that taking days off work isn't really possible, and no matter how crap I've felt at times over the last few years I've always managed to make it in even if I'm crawling. On this occasion I hoped that it would just be a bad morning or day and that tomorrow I'd be fine and able to get my long cycle in. How wrong was I? The weekend came and went and unfortunately my MS symptoms were quite debilitating and I couldn't train. I missed five full days of training, and with me due to board a plane in just over a week, this was less than ideal – actually, that's an understatement. It was Wednesday before things settled with my body and I was back out training again. I told my subconscious that the rest had done me good, and that a few days off training at the end of an intense six-month programme probably wouldn't do too much harm. Over the next week I got back in my routine; thankfully my six-month Ironman training was coming to a close. The great news was that I'd completed five events in the last eighteen weeks, stuck with my nutritional plan and exceeded all my own lofty expectations. Crucially, bearing in mind the scale of the challenges I'd set myself, I'd avoided a serious injury, which was a terrific bonus.

I was really looking forward to my trip, and over the next few days I put the finishing touches to my plan and made sure all of my equipment was primed and ready to go. There was a total of ten travelling with me to Majorca, including my two children, and Team Devine was now very excited and more importantly ready. A few months earlier I'd booked an excellent hotel in Alcúdia, the north of the island. If you're competing in an event like this, it's important that everything is meticulously planned: travel, equipment, accommodation, food and rest. All of these contribute to how you'll perform on the day, so I spent some time making sure everything was in order. Not only did I want to be well-prepared for the race, I wanted to make sure my family had a terrific time too. The hard work was now complete, and it was time to relax and prepare myself mentally for what lay ahead. The dream was becoming a reality.

Adventure

I left my family home at eighteen and set sail for university – my first proper adventure in life, and what an adventure it turned out to be as I'm sure anyone who has experienced university would concur. Since then adventure has been a constant theme in my life, and in the last twenty years I've found travelling to be an important contributor to my personal development in the skills I've acquired. I've found that adventure comes with travelling through the journey of life, with adventure comes adversity and with adversity comes growth. When I sat down at Christmas 2014 to set my challenges – challenges that would stretch and push me beyond anything I'd done before – I knew that an Ironman was the one thing that scared the hell out of me. The more I looked into it, the more challenging and frightening it became; however, something else happened too: subconsciously I wanted to take that challenge on. I can't really explain it but that's how I felt at the time. Over the last six months I'd worked my backside off to get my mind and body into such a shape that meant I would finish this bloody thing alive. If I could do this, I knew my life would change forever.

In a few days' time, all of the talking, training, worrying and plotting would be over. I'd be standing on a beach in Majorca waiting for the starter's gun with just over one hundred and forty-six miles between me and the finishing line. The big question was, would I finish and become that iron man I thought was impossible not that long ago?

Alcúdia

We arrived in Alcúdia on a beautiful Thursday evening at sundown. Anyone who has had the pleasure of visiting this amazing little island will agree it's a picture.

The resort we stayed in was a couple of miles outside the village of Alcúdia, and it had everything I needed down to a massage tent which I became very familiar with over the next few days. My plan was to take it easy on Friday, maybe do some swimming in the pool, eat plenty of nutritious food and read, and, as luck would have it, I did just that. The other matter I had to navigate was my two children, Lilyanna and Conor Junior, who were absolutely buzzing being away on their holidays. This made the whole experience that much more fulfilling as I couldn't think of anything better than to complete one of the hardest endurance challenges known to man only to be greeted by my nearest and dearest, especially my two prized possessions.

Saturday was an important day because I would register for the event, go to the race briefing and suck up the atmosphere that is Ironman. The briefing was at midday, and with just under three thousand athletes in attendance, there would be some excitement around base camp. I cycled the ten kilometres to registration early on Saturday morning and from one kilometre away I could hear the buzz and music bouncing out from the sound systems at the beachfront. It was a hive of anticipation with loads of people, smiling faces, families, iron men and fellow athletes all in great form. I registered early to miss the queue, which I highly recommend if you're ever competing in an Ironman. After some retail therapy in the Ironman store I wandered over to the race briefing to get a good seat. It was scheduled to last an hour and there were two other briefings, one in German and one in French, immediately afterwards. I was overawed by the sheer scale of the event, and what struck me most was the professionalism, the organisation and the overarching sense of fun that was in the air. It felt amazing to be a part of it all.

At twelve on the button a roar went up as legendary Ironman announcer Paul Kaye took to the stage to welcome all of us crazies to the beautiful island of Majorca. The Ironman Majorca 2015 briefing was about to begin, and the crowd roared its approval as Kaye went into his now-familiar routine of delivering the rules and regulations of the race kicking off in less than twenty-four hours. It's vital to get to the race briefing in good time and listen to what you're being told. I spent most of my time lapping up the atmosphere, looking around me and admiring my fellow competitors so incredulous was I to be surrounded by such a unique bunch of people. I tuned in and out of Kaye's talk, and I heard something about the mountain climb, part of the bike course in tomorrow's race. I was aware there was a bit of a climb with the bike as I'd read it online and saw the map, and I knew it would be a tough-enough test, but Kaye made light of it, calling it a 'little hill' which got a few laughs from the crowd. I wasn't too bothered because my training was done and I knew I wasn't going to get any stronger twenty-four hours before the race, so there was little point in worrying.

The briefing came to an end and I made my way back to the hotel to chill-out in the sun with my family, get some good food in me and hopefully a massage if I could fit it in. That afternoon was great. My family were all relaxed and enjoying the sun-kissed island, and with many fellow ath-letes staying at the same hotel, there was a great buzz with preparations in abundance for the race tomorrow. Late afternoon, I spotted a very fit guy in the pool who looked like he was also racing. I introduced myself and we had a chat. Michael, as I thought, was in town for the race. More interest-ing though, he was from Greece, and was the captain of a NATO warship. I should have known because of his physique and due to the fact he was glid-ing through the pool like a submarine. This was his first Ironman too and he was as excited as I was with what the next day would hold. We had a great chat over the next hour or so, and it was really nice to share our thoughts on the race, training and life in general. Michael was extremely focused and very composed – qualities I've found that are a common thread in people who compete in challenges of this type.

Early evening I went back to my room and dressed for dinner. As it was the night before race day I wanted to ensure I got plenty of nutritious food into my body. Fish was a constant on my plate along with rice, salad and pasta, all of which formed my last supper.

The children were in great form that evening, and I was so busy making sure young Conor didn't have more than three bowls of ice cream I didn't have time to think about the race. My sister and her husband were arriving that evening and I was really looking forward to seeing them. It made the whole event more special having most of the family in attendance and all in great spirits. My mum was keeping the wee ones in her room that night as I needed to be well-rested for what was going to be a very tough day to-morrow. As I lay in bed thinking about the race, a text came through from Luke Tyburski. He told me to smile tomorrow, congratulated me for getting to the start line, and told me to remember that my Ironman was already complete. He suggested that the training of the last six months was the actual Ironman, and that tomorrow would be my glory lap where I should take in the atmosphere, applause and excitement and treat the event as a celebration. I read the text over and over again and it flicked a switch in my brain, I knew he was right. I had knocked my pan in over the last number of months, had completed five of the six events I had set myself, kept going, stuck with my plan and here I was twenty-four hours from the finishing line. This was just the psychology and message I needed to receive, so, Luke – thanks very much, champ.

Race Day

I was super excited going to bed and subsequently didn't get the best night's sleep, but thankfully I managed a few hours' shut-eye. My alarm went off at four forty-five, and, although still the middle of the night as far as I was concerned, after a few seconds I jumped out of bed and dressed. Breakfast was at five fifteen, so I needed to be regimented from here on in, get the game head on and focus for the day ahead. The hotel restaurant was already a hive of activity with athletes tucking in and making sure they had enough fuel on board for the grueling test to come.

The bus to transition was very quiet because most of us were still half-asleep. It was peaceful and I got a sense of calm and fulfillment coming over me which I can't explain. I had some quiet time, just me and my thoughts, thankful I'd arrived in Alcúdia in one piece. It was a nice feeling getting to the starting line in decent shape, and most of all calm. The bus pulled up outside transition and I went to check on my bike and see that my tyres had enough pressure in them. Yesterday, when I dropped my bike off, I let the pressure out of my tyres as recommended by other athletes whose bikes were beside mine. Apparently in the heat the tyres can expand and in some cases explode, which wouldn't be a great find at six o clock the morning of a race. I didn't take any chances and so had to pump them back up. With the race due to start at eight, I had an hour to get sorted and make my way to the beach. There were thousands of athletes doing last-minute preparations and huge numbers of friends and family stationed outside transition supporting their nearest and dearest in the big race. The morning of an

Ironman is incredible – it's hard to put into words, and is an experience I won't forget for a very long time.

Around seven thirty I had my wetsuit on and was advised, with the other athletes, to make my way to the beachfront for the 8 a.m. start. I was met by my family who had got up at stupid o'clock to come down and see me off – a really nice touch which made everything worthwhile, and with such a daunting challenge ahead, their familiar faces in crowds of thousands were a welcome sight. At ten to eight Paul Kaye announced that he wanted all of us over to the starting line. This was it. No pulling out now. All the training and talking was over and the race was about to start. It was a terrific moment to watch the sun rising from the west to overlook Alcúdia Bay; it was truly a sight to behold. I was surprisingly calm but excited to get going. Although I wasn't a great swimmer, I was satisfied I would get through the swim if I stuck with my plan of concentrating on my technique and rotating my arms. Discipline, desire, sheer grit and more discipline would get me through the swim and the rest of the day.

Starter's Gun

Eight on the button and we were off to the sound of the starter's gun. It was a rolling start, which suited me great, so I walked very slowly into the sea – just as I'd done in my previous races – and when the water reached my waist, I was off. My race had begun. Like before, my strategy was to stay well away from the crowd, find my rhythm and take my time. I thought that if I kept out to the left, I would be ok, and that's what I did. I progressed north out of the bay as the amazing sunrise continued to the west. With just under three thousand athletes in the water, from above it must have looked like the world's biggest washing machine. I made steady progress lifting my head to breathe every three strokes, a technique I'd practised in training which was working out fine for me on race day.

When I'm swimming I try and think of positive situations in my life to keep my mind focused on the job ahead. If you're like me and you're not a swimmer, it can be quite boring, so from a mental-health perspective my positive-thought process I'd been perfecting in the previous months was bearing fruit. I expected to be in the water well over an hour and ten minutes, so I self-talked to stay relaxed, kept breathing in time and kept the strokes coming one after another. After an hour and twenty-one minutes, I finished the longest open-water swim I'd ever attempted – a terrific feeling. I was certainly tired as I walked from the shoreline, but there was no time for rest and I broke into a slow jog to transition to ready myself for the 112-mile cycle in the heat of the Majorcan sun. I felt tremendous leaving the water and my family were in great spirits, thrilled to see me come out of the water alive, I'm sure – my mum in particular, who'd probably said three full rosaries during the time I was in the sea.

My race plan was to take my time in transition, steady up, get some fuel into me and then head off on the bike. My ultimate goal was genuinely to finish alive and within the time allowed, eighteen hours, so I wasn't remotely interested in rushing myself through transition. I felt quite strong as I wrestled with my wetsuit and got into my bike gear. I felt incredible having mastered the swim and mentally I was in a really good place. There was a tremendous buzz in transition getting ready with other athletes for what was going to be one very long and difficult day. Finally I was ready to go, so off I set to the roars of the crowds lining the streets of Alcúdia cheering me and my fellow athletes on and making the whole thing extra special.

It was approaching half ten and I was ten miles into the cycle. The weather was beautiful and I was relaxed and enjoying myself. I planned to eat every thirty minutes on the bike – as I'd done in Dublin a few weeks earlier – to ensure I'd enough fuel on board to get me round in one piece. All the research I'd read had placed extreme importance on fuelling at the right time and not waiting till I was hungry or my race may be over. My nutrition needed to be bang on, especially given the expected hot conditions.

The bike course was absolutely beautiful, and I made my way south through some of the most picturesque villages I'd ever seen. In front of me I noticed a fellow competitor with an Irish flag on her back. I came up alongside her and, to make her feel at home, shouted over in my Tyrone tongue;

'How's it going there?' - I think I got her on the hop – in the middle of Majorca she probably didn't expect someone from home pulling up alongside her. She introduced herself as Ciara Donnelly, a Tyrone local too, and over the next twenty miles or so we had a great chat about all things Ironman and life in general. Ciara was one tough cookie, and, as with everyone who enters Ironman, had her own story which was hugely impressive and inspirational: she'd had a baby eighteen months previous and this was her first ever triathlon if you don't mind. An incredible accomplishment, and being from a small village in Co. Tyrone I never doubted the strength and desire of the woman.

Around mile fifty I pushed on a little and chatted to other athletes as we cycled alongside each other. Each one shared their own incredible story and reasons for competing which made the cycle go that much faster. The camaraderie was tremendous and the mutual respect between us athletes was evident.

The Mountain

Around mile seventy I was cruising at seventeen miles per hour up a slight incline, fairly steady, and I could see ahead of me the beginning of the climb for the 'little hill', to quote Paul Kaye. I was cycling blind because I hadn't driven the bike course yesterday, which in hindsight I should have done and which experienced Ironman athletes will tell you to do so you know what you're up against. I didn't have the time to do it yesterday, so I would just have to see what surprises the 'little hill' brought.

About mile seventy-five I was getting it tight. The gradient of the so-called 'little hill' was increasing and I was now in the middle of a full-on mountain ascent, for fuck's sake, and not enjoying it one bit. The sweat ran down my face, and the mountain got steadily steeper. The only consolation was that everyone appeared to be in the same level of pain. Forty-five minutes later, still quite a bit away from the top, all I could think about was Paul Kaye at the briefing the day before talking of the 'easy climb'. He was clearly taking the piss, and at this point of the race I didn't find it particularly funny at all. I was struggling for the first time in the race with my wheels just about turning in spite of the steepness of the climb and my legs burning like crazy craving a piece of downhill action. After an hour and fifteen minutes of climbing, I saw the top of the mountain for the first time, and, more importantly, a Portaloo at the side of the road. I jumped off, stretched my legs and went to the toilet. I had a drink and ate the remainder of a bar to get some much-needed fuel on board, and while I was doing that I noticed a large number of people congregated at the junction a few hundred yards up the road. Delighted at having finally broken the back of this bloody mountain, I got back on my bike and cracked on with the race.

Your Race is Over

As I reached the junction at the top of the hill, I immediately realised something was badly wrong. Athletes were off their bikes, many of them visibly angry with some even crying. Out of nowhere a guy came over and asked for my name. I told him and he said that my race was over, that I was out of the event. The exchange went as follows:

Race Marshal: What is your name?
CD: Conor Devine.
RM: Your race is over, sir. I'm sorry.
CD: What are you talking about?
RM: Your race is over. Fifteen hundred hours was the cut-off to get to this point in the course, and you are eleven minutes over.

CD: What the hell are you talking about? I have eight hours to complete the bike course – that's the Ironman rules!
RM: Go away. It's over, I'm sorry.
CD: What do you mean you're sorry? What the hell is going on here?

I turned to a few of the athletes standing next to me – some too distressed to talk – and asked what was going on. Apparently at the race briefing yesterday, while I was looking around me thinking I was King fucking Kong, Paul Kaye said that we had to be at the top of the mountain by 3 p.m. Clearly I hadn't heard him or I would have made sure I made the time, however what was I going to do now? I was absolutely fuming. There was no fucking way I was out of this race. I trained for seven months to get here and I didn't need some ignorant tosser telling me I was out of the race. To my mind the Ironman rules were very clear: I had eight hours to complete the bike and seventeen hours to complete the race in total. It became obvious that everyone around me had given up and accepted their race was over. I sat there almost crying and deliberated my next move. All sorts of thoughts were running through my mind: what would I tell my family? I was a failure. I wasn't strong enough, and the race was just too big for me. The Big Bad Wolf inside was telling me to forget it and give up; however, my heart was saying, 'Fuck it, get back on your bike and keep going, Conor, for Christ's sake. If you can get to transition before eight hours, they might let you continue the race.' After a few more agonising minutes, that's exactly what I did.

Back on the saddle like a man possessed, I cycled through the crowd and headed for Alcúdia on my own. I knew there was approximately thirty-five miles to go, and if I kept my foot on the gas, I could get there under the eight hours allocated for the cycle. I was absolutely devastated I was on my own with not a fellow athlete in sight. Everyone who had reached the junction after 3 p.m. had given up, their race over. Even the fucking water stations had packed up as I was closing in on Alcudia and were no longer on this part of the course. It was then that I slipped into a real dark space mentally, my head was wrecked. I cycled in the heat on my own for miles, and with each rotation of the pedals the negative thoughts in my head were getting the better of me – maybe my race was over, what exactly am I doing?

However, (and I don't know how), there was a small flame flickering in my heart, encouraging me to keep going, that told me I might be ok. I was just fifteen miles from transition when I decided to get my game head back on and hammer the life out of the pedals. About a mile in front of me I spotted Ciara Donnelly again – how the hell did she pass me anyway? I caught up with her and she confirmed that we were out of the race.

'Fuck it, Ciara, keep going. They're wrong. You just never know, we might be ok.'

And that's what we did. The next twenty-five minutes were the toughest I'd faced in a very long time, my head all over the joint, not to mention that I'd cycled nearly one hundred miles in roaring heat and was nine hours into an endurance race with every bone in my body squealing with pain.

I entered Alcúdia and the crowds were out in full force. There were no other athletes in sight, so they appeared to be cheering me on to transition, which felt incredible. The next few minutes were crucial as I would find out my fate in the race. I pulled up at transition, and I could see it had taken me seven hours and fifty-two minutes on the timing board. I was eight minutes within the Ironman threshold and was hoping they would let me through. As I entered transition two, I was very nervous, not to mention exhausted, and called out to one of the race marshals to check if it was ok for me to carry on in the race. He was very helpful and radioed through to the control centre. After a couple of minutes, which felt more like an hour, he yelled out, 'Señor, yes, continue, please. You are still in the race.'

'Fuck me.' I couldn't believe what I was hearing. All of a sudden these feelings of anger and utopia came over me at the same time. Anger that that tosser at the top of the hill had nearly ruined my Ironman dream and utopia that I was still in the race. Boom! I was running through transition to change into my running gear when I heard a couple of guys shouting my name like two crazy idiots. I looked over the fence to see my brother, Colm, and brother-in-law, Jonny, who had both obviously been enjoying some of the local beer houses over the last few hours, as I was cycling over one hundred miles in the roaring heat.

'Go on, Conor. Keep going. You can do it" they shouted not in any kind of harmony I must add but certainly had the desired effect.

That was exactly the motivation and encouragement I needed. From the hundreds of bikes lined up I gathered that the majority of athletes had already been through transition, but I couldn't have cared less. All that concerned me now was nailing the marathon and becoming the Ironman I had thought impossible. As I left transition and made my way out to start the run, tears of accomplishment, pain, happiness and downright gratefulness trickled down my face. I knew I had broken the back of this thing now and if I took my time on the run, I would get round. It was an incredible feeling.

The Run

It was just before 6 p.m. and I'd been on the course some ten hours. I worked out in my head that even if I walked half the marathon and ran the other half, I would still finish on time, and for the first time in the race I was pretty certain I would complete it. But for anyone who has ran a marathon, a great achievement in itself, it's a very difficult challenge, so I was aware I needed to stick rigidly to my plan of eating and drinking every half hour and thinking good thoughts.

The marathon course was terrific: four laps of Alcúdia town centre. There were thousands of cheering supporters the whole way round, and it was a tremendous feeling and a much-welcome boost to my morale. My marathon plan was to jog quite slowly, take it easy and suck everything up. Although it was heading into early evening, it was still very hot and I needed to get as many fluids into my body as possible. The first few miles weren't so bad as I was probably running on adrenaline and the atmosphere of the crowd. Approaching the first-lap marker I noticed the marshals were handing out coloured wristbands but I wasn't too sure why. It then dawned on me that this was to remind us runners of how far we had ran and maybe to make sure we didn't do more than the 26.2 miles – no harm to the Ironman team, but if this was the reason for the wristbands, rest assured I wouldn't be going over the set miles, thanks very much.

Ten miles into the run and I was still taking things quite slowly. I noticed just up ahead of me one unfortunate athlete being taken away in an ambulance. I'm not sure what happened, but it was more than likely due to dehydration. In any case, that athlete's race was over. A mile or two further up the road I saw another two athletes taken off the course by first-aiders with one put straight into an ambulance. Again, unfortunately for them, their races were over. Seeing athletes in this shape reminded me of how serious a challenge an Ironman is with the pressure and stress it puts on the body.

At nearly eight thirty in the evening, with the sun starting to go down, I was halfway through the marathon. Looking around me, the setting was amazing. The town was a picture, and it was a real honour to be running around it with so many champions. Physically I was beginning to struggle. My legs were sore all over and my mind was weakening. Around mile eighteen I did something I've never had to do before: I asked myself some questions. It's hard to explain but I was feeling very present, even spiritual, and despite being in so much pain and being so tired I wanted to create an environment in my head where I was only grateful for everything that was good in my life. I thought about my children, my family, my business, my health, taking part in such an iconic event, along with some positive thoughts. Although I had some difficult situations going on in my life at that time, when I set it out in my head it was clear that I had more to be thankful for. This conversation in my head was a regular occurrence over the remaining six miles of the marathon. I knew if I was to finish the race, it was incredibly important that my mind was strong and I was convinced that if that was the case then my body would follow.

I was at mile twenty-four just after ten o'clock in the evening. I'd been on the course some fourteen and a half hours, and with just over two miles to go I was going to achieve my goal. One foot in front of the other, one foot in front of the other, one foot in front of the other – this was my self-talk for the last twenty minutes of the marathon. My energy levels, although completely exhausted, appeared to be ok all things considering, and with five hundred metres to go, I felt absolutely exhilarated. Up in front of me I could hear Paul Kaye call out each athlete's name and the country they were representing as they crossed the finishing line. Now I was ready to hear mine. With a couple of hundred yards to go I saw my family who had been out all day supporting me, willing me to the finishing line. It was an incredible feeling to see them right at the end of this mammoth challenge. I turned the last corner, only one hundred metres from home, with the crowd in great spirits and the music pumping. I saw Paul readying himself to welcome me, and, all of a sudden, as I hit the magic carpet:

CONOR DEVINE, YOU ARE AN IRONMAN

About ten metres from the finishing line, my young daughter, Lilyanna, jumped the barrier and ran over to me. It was an amazing touch for both of us to cross the line of Alcúdia Ironman 2015 together, even if it wasn't planned. I was completely overwhelmed and was lost for words. I'd been on the course a grand total of fifteen hours and five minutes and had finally achieved my goal – in fact, something much bigger than my goal, but the only thing I thought of at that point was that I needed to sit down, as I was completely exhausted.

I walked over to the rest zone and was handed a warm blanket and a glass of Coca-Cola while being warmly greeted by my family. Everyone was delighted with what I'd achieved and were very grateful to see me cross the line in one piece. Only Conor Junior, my young son asleep in his pram, passed no remarks. The wee man looked more wrecked than me having been out in the sun all day waiting to see his dad finish safe and sound. It was a terrific feeling to finally get some rest and to chat with my family and admire the huge medal I had just been handed. I'd done it, achieved the impossible and lived to tell the tale. I was extremely proud of myself over the last fifteen hours, and had a feeling of amazement, that will live with me for a very long time. My race was over, I was well and truly exhausted and I needed to rest. Something I knew for certain was I would sleep like a baby tonight, sorry, an Ironman.

CHAPTER 9

My neurologist told me I needed to quit my
job and stop playing football. I decided to set
up my own business and do an Ironman.

CONOR DEVINE

Never Give Up

I remember the following exchanges like yesterday;

> Dr. Watt: 'Conor, you have MS and I recommend you get on a dis-
> ease modifying drug as soon as possible.'
> CD: 'Ok, which one do you recommend?'
> Dr. Watt: 'It's up to you. There are four options. You could try one
> and see how it goes?'
> CD: 'Ok, I'll give Rebif a go.'

The above exchange was like an out-of-body experience in 2007. I couldn't believe what was happening to me. As already stated it was an incredibly difficult
and surreal time in my life. I remember asking Dr. Watt did he think I would
play football again to which he resolutely said no, and furthermore he stated

that I may need to consider other forms of employment as MS can be pretty debilitating and isn't conducive to stress or work which is very intensive.

I'm now living ten years with MS, and thankfully I didn't listen to all of the negative claptrap that often comes with hardships and illnesses. I won't lie to you: it's been an incredibly difficult time for me. The way I've dealt with it over the years is by keeping my bad days and hard times to myself. Like lots of people in similar circumstances, I felt for long periods that I didn't really have anyone to talk to about it anyway and it's just something I had to come to terms with. I'm still a young man and could never have dreamed how my life would pan out over the past ten years. Without getting into it in any real detail – I like to keep some of my personal life completely personal – the MS along with other traumatic situations have created a huge amount of adversity for me to manage and live with; I recently described to a good friend how I felt my life was similar to running through hell. I've come to understand, and more so accept, that life throws so many challenges at you that it makes it incredibly difficult and even cruel at times, and there have been plenty of occasions when I've thought of throwing in the towel. What I also now understand is that despite the setbacks and falling over, it's important to get back on your feet and go again – just like the old Chinese proverb I say to myself constantly: fall down seven times, get up eight. The Ironman journey with the training, discipline and planning required fitted in very well with how I've led my life over the past few years. Yes, it was incredibly painful, required huge amounts of effort, grit, perseverance and resilience to get to the finishing line in one piece, but seeing my family's proud faces on the marathon run in Majorca was so empowering, and crossing the finishing line with my daughter was absolutely priceless.

Triathlon is one of the fastest growing sports across the world, and Ironman itself is going from strength to strength. There's no doubt that it's an incredible test of character for anyone to undertake such a challenge, and I'm grateful that despite my MS and everything else going on, I faced this, five other events and completed them all in twenty weeks smashing my Against

All Odds campaign and in doing so raised awareness of MS worldwide. I also raised a lot of money for the MS Society, but, more importantly, gave myself a huge confidence boost that despite setbacks with the right mix of ingredients I can achieve my dreams and overcome whatever life throws at me.

One of the motivations for writing this book was to let you into my mind for a period to virtually travel with me through 2015 until I crossed the finishing line in Majorca. I'm incredibly stoked that I've helped and encouraged so many people to believe in themselves by completing this challenge. It's very important to me that you challenge yourself and get outside your comfort zone. At one point, not that long ago, I thought there was no chance of me ever doing a sprint triathlon never mind an Ironman, but I expanded my mind and allowed myself to believe that if I applied myself and put in the work, I could achieve my dream. I believe this can happen no matter what challenges or goals you set yourself. If you want to achieve something in life, it's important that firstly you allow your mind to believe, even just for a few moments, that it's possible to achieve that dream. I truly believe that all of us can develop an iron mind that will allow us to realise our potential, and if there's one thing my story does for you, surely it's that you agree with me on this. To drill into this a little further, for your own benefit, I'll now set out the tools you need in your locker to develop an iron mindset which will allow you to reach your goals in life.

Ingredients

To develop the iron mindset which will allow you to realise your potential, there are ingredients you need to find, understand and work out how to bring them into your life. There hasn't been a subject studied more in the last hundred years than success. If you type 'success' into Google, you could spend months going through thousands of papers on what defines success. The fact that you're reading this book tells me you're already on your way to developing an iron mindset. I truly believe that no matter what challenges you face in life, if you can manage your thoughts, are disciplined, work hard and allow your mind to expand to believe what you're asking it to do, you can achieve anything. So many people consciously decide to play it safe in life. Not because they're enjoying it, but because they're afraid to push themselves and leave their comfort zone. When I was diagnosed with multiple sclerosis aged twenty-eight it was tough going. My dreams and aspirations went up in smoke almost immediately. I faced a huge wall and felt like I had nowhere to turn. It was a defining moment in my life. You too will have moments like this to deal with, but hopefully you might be able to take something from me sharing my experiences, to allow you to believe that everything is possible. It's important to understand that it's not the problem you have to get your head round, it's how you react to it that matters. Who would have thought someone with MS would be racing in an Ironman? Surely that's not possible, right? Look into it and see how many people across the world have achieved this feat. I've looked, and from what I can see there aren't too many folk out there, but that's not what's important, what's important is that I believed it was possible, put a plan in place and worked exceptionally hard to achieve my dream which in five months got me to the starting line in Majorca. I'm more than proud of my achievements and the profound effect it's had on me, those closest to me and other people who need a little encouragement. I'm now constantly trying to encourage people to get off the floor and fight back against adversity. I encourage everyone to reject what they're led to believe by family, friends, doctors, media and anyone else who has an opinion on what can and can't be achieved in life. We all need to remember that it's us as individuals who go on to create our own reality not anyone else or the situations or unfortunate circumstances we meet that shape us. It's true that without dreams people perish. It's imperative we all have goals that inspire our hearts and souls, that make us feel alive. Ask yourself if you're really living or if you're simply alive? There's a huge difference, but thankfully I'm now truly living.

Goals

Over the last few years I've immersed myself in personal development. I've begun exercising my brain by reading, listening to podcasts, speaking with people who I admire and learning from others what practices they embrace which allow them to not only survive but also thrive.

Will Smith, the American actor, is someone I admire a lot. He says not to try and reinvent the wheel as it's very likely that whatever you're trying to do has already been done. In relating that to Ironman Majorca, one of the first things I did was get on the Internet to learn as much as I could about the race and its requirements. There was so much to learn from previous competitors that there was no need for me to start from scratch with a plan, to reinvent the wheel, if you like. To work out whether it was an achievable goal I needed to understand what the dangers were, the fitness requirements, the role and importance of nutrition among a shedload of other relevant information. Over an eight-week period I gleaned so much information on the race that the idea of competing in an event myself became possible in my head.

The work of the American philosopher Jim Rohn and writer Napoleon Hill really sold me on the importance of setting goals to progress in life. Up until I was twenty-eight years old, I never wrote down any goals that I wanted to achieve. Of course I had thoughts in my head of what I wanted to do and become, but I never drilled into them, wrote them down and fully focused on achieving them. When I sat down in December 2014 and wrote out my goals for the twelve months ahead, the Ironman was there in black and white. This meant that I was serious about the challenge, and the next step was focusing on how I was going to achieve it.

For anyone contemplating any form of success, it's crucial that you get into this frame of mind and write down your goals. I do this religiously every year between Boxing Day and New Year's Eve. I now look forward to it and year-on-year continue to stretch my mind to ensure I grow and get outside my comfort zone. Goals are the start of achieving any dream and are key ingredients to your overall philosophy.

Nutrition and exercise play a pivotal role in my life now. I tend to focus a lot of my goals around them – the reason being that I know if I'm getting the right nutrients in, my mind and body will work to maximum potential. If I then stick to my exercise and adventure goals, clearly I can be the best version of me. This is where it's at with me now. I'm always asking how I can be a better version of me, how I can reach my potential. These are the kinds of questions you should be asking yourself every morning too. What am I going to do better today than yesterday? How can I add more value to the people I'm with today, the business I'm building, how much more can I give in the gym or in the conversations I have with staff, friends and family. This is now a way of life and plays such an important role in how I set out my stall each day, week and month.

If you want to get on in life, it's essential to set goals: short, medium and long-term goals that are a mixture of health, business and family-related goals. Whatever they are is your choice, but make sure they encompass these three things:

- They are achievable.
- They get you out of your comfort zone.
- At least one of them scares you.

Structured Plan

No matter what your goals or aspirations are in life, you won't hit too many of them if you don't have a coordinated plan in place. From a youngster I've always been fairly self-sufficient. Mum and Dad woke me for school every morning, but for as long as I can remember I got up, dressed myself and looked forward to the day ahead. Sport played a very influential role in my life as it dictated the environment I grew up in from an early age. One of the huge benefits from playing in teams at such a young age is that I was always working to some kind of plan, trying to help both myself and others in my team win football matches. This resulted in me being familiar with setting goals and aware of the importance of planning to achieve any kind of dream or goal.

If you've decided to do your first 10k run, it's likely that to avoid injury and achieve your goal, you'll need to work to some kind of structured plan. In this day and age there's so much information available around running that you've no excuse not to tailor the right plan for you. This is a key aspect to any plan: research and then work to a plan that matches your own capabilities. For my Ironman I was very aware that I needed to firstly increase my knowledge of the event and get a complete understanding what was required if I was to finish the damn thing alive. I was mindful of how dangerous the race could be if I wasn't properly prepared, and it would have been completely irresponsible of me not to give the challenge the respect it deserved. So I read numerous books, journals, spoke to people who had competed at that level and tried to gain an understanding of what was actually involved. Once I completed this part of the planning, I programmed myself to develop a mindset that such a lofty challenge was achievable. I then developed a rigorous training plan which included six events which complemented each other and would be greatly beneficial to the challenge.

There are a number of reasons why you need to have a structured plan in place for whatever challenge you set yourself. I've shared some thoughts on this with you below:

- Planning helps overall decision-making; it allows you to research whatever your goals are which enables you to make the right decisions in life.
- Planning encourages you to be creative with your thoughts and goals.
- Planning helps you maintain control on your progress.

- Planning greatly reduces the risk of injury or of failing to achieve your goals and ambitions in life.
- A goal without any kind of plan is merely a pipe dream.

Discipline

The *Oxford English Dictionary* defines discipline as 'the practice of training people to obey rules or a code of behaviour, using punishment to correct disobedience'. Discipline is a key ingredient if you want to develop an iron mindset. People often ask me, 'How the hell will you do that race?' I always tell them the same thing: if you do the training, stay focused and are disciplined, then you too could achieve this goal. I meet so many people and have a lot of friends who simply don't have enough discipline in their lives. This results in them losing focus and dropping goals that negatively impact them, their health, their relationships and their businesses. This is a real turn-off for me as the majority of people don't know they're living, and they simply don't have the work ethic or desire to achieve their potential. I can tell you now, if you're not disciplined, then an Ironman isn't the challenge for you. Think about something else: a marathon, Olympic triathlon or something a lot easier in terms of the commitment and effort required. The commitment and effort I needed to put in to my Ironman was one of the most attractive parts of the challenge. I knew that if I could complete the training programme, just as Luke said, the actual Ironman event is the glory lap.

My life has been very disciplined from the get-go. Playing football from a very young age and being involved with team environments for long periods shaped me. It was absolutely a challenge for me to train six days a week, look after my young family, build a business and manage my own health and well-being. Even the very thought of it was spine tingling, but I wanted it enough to go for it. And if you can combine discipline with hard work and desire, then I'm telling you now, you'll be unstoppable.

Resolve

The best definition of resolve that I've ever heard came from a young girl about twelve years of age who was asked to explain it. Her response was, '*I think this is where you promise yourself to never give up.*' I think this defines resolve beautifully. It's an outstanding quality for any human to acquire, and if you want to develop an iron mindset, you'll need this in abundance. At the beginning of my MS journey I struggled with this, and, in fact, I didn't have any resolve at all as I'd given up on life and myself; it was a very tough time. But, guess what? I hung in there, started to exercise and eat nutritious food, and what do you think happened? Things started to change. Throughout that hellish experience, I promised myself that one day, when I eventually got strong enough, I was never going to give up on anything ever again.

There are people out there who practise resolve every day and go on to achieve champion status. They've taken all of what life has thrown at them and then some but continue to step forward. Recently I met a guy called Frank who was eighty-two years old. Frank looked great, very fit and full of conversation. I asked him what his secret was. He told me he had led a very positive eighty-two years, but that it had been extremely tough and laced with adversity. His wife dying of cancer a few years back shook him greatly, and just over thirty years ago his youngest son took his own life, which he was yet to truly get over. We were chatting away like old schoolmates so intrigued was I by Frank, his courage and his resolve. Frank had no notion of slowing down and walked three miles every morning at seven o'clock and had a wee brandy every night at nine o'clock. He had six children, five still alive, and had a lot of problems to deal with over the years. Frank continues to drive forward and leads a positive and active life. There is absolutely no doubt that Frank has developed an iron mindset over the last eighty-two years. In terms of resolve, well, Frank walks and talks it. There's no question about it. But, even more importantly, he's a great guy.

Be Thankful

Every morning when I wake up I'm thankful. That sounds a little cliché, but it's where I am in my life. I've had to rewire my brain over the last few years, change my thought processes and take responsibility for my circumstances. I've read well over a hundred books in the last four years, and in that time frame I've learned to live more in the moment and become a lot more thankful for everything I have in life. Trust me, I've many challenges to deal with on a daily basis and being a lot more thankful, and indeed thoughtful, has made me mentally tougher. If you speak to others who have put themselves through Ironman challenges and other extreme adventures, I'm sure a lot of them would tell you that your state of mind is key to survival and fulfillment. There would be absolutely no merit in training for an Ironman if you were in a bad frame of mind. It's crucially important to have the ability to control what goes on between your ears and to be thankful for all the good things that have happened in your life and are continuing to happen.

When I was running the marathon leg of Ironman Majorca suffering excruciating pain all over my body, I focused on all the good things happening in my life. I was extremely thankful that I was in a position to actually compete in such an event. This helped me a lot during the very tough parts of the race, the parts when I wanted to give up, stop and throw in the towel. Reflecting and being thankful in life is another key ingredient to developing an iron mindset. The Ironman has been a very rewarding experience for me. Through completing it I've inspired a few people to eat better, train harder and set goals. Life is one long, hard, slow climb, but if you seek out challenges and opportunities and surround yourself with people who genuinely love and care for you, you will continue to make progress.

Jim Rohn, who I mentioned above, has had a huge impact on my life. I never got to meet Jim but his philosophy, books, talks and behaviour have added significant value to me and how I've lived my life over the past ten years. I've read many of his books and it's incredible how effective his content is and, more so, how it helped me develop an iron mindset that was influential in getting me across the Ironman finishing line as well as helping me accomplish other things in my life. It's a truly wonderful experience to listen to Jim or read some of his work.

As we all get a little older we become a lot more experienced in life. If we commit to equipping ourselves with more skills then our goals and our aspirations we have for ourselves and our families become a lot more achievable. Personal development has been a constant in my life for quite some time now and below I have taken this opportunity to share with you some of my thoughts on how we can all start to go on and become better versions of ourselves.

- LET'S DO IT – Talk is cheap. If you set yourself a goal in life, work out a plan to get you there, then make a decision and say to yourself "lets do it" and repeat it over and over again. An extremely powerful approach and ingredient to achieve anything in life.

- ASK FOR ADVENTURE – How many people do you know play it safe? I would say it's ninety-eight per cent of everyone I know. Many people don't like their jobs but for one reason or another they stay in those same jobs for twenty years. It's incredible and at times mind-blowing, but you know it's true. So ask for adventure, push the boundaries because everything in life is risky. The one truth about life is that none of us are going to get out of here alive, so why not change your attitude and give it a go. If you live your life in the comfort zone and crave security, to my mind you won't have a very fulfilling life.

- WORK ON YOURSELF - If you work harder on yourself than you do on your job, your life will begin to improve. Many have suggested if you work hard on your job, you will make a living, but if you work harder on yourself, you have the potential to make a fortune and live the life of your dreams. I hadn't a clue what personal development was all about until I turned twenty-eight. Once I started this process and committed to the programme of development over the last twelve years, I've been able to turn my life and my health around. If you are genuine about developing an iron mindset, then you must commit to working on all aspects of yourself.

- HAVE A PURPOSE – If you have a clear list of priorities and a purpose in your life, then the law of attraction can pull you through your challenges and goals. I really wanted to become that Ironman because I knew it would have an incredible impact on myself and others. This purpose allowed me to develop the mindset I required to get me over the finish line. Often what you will find is that if your purpose doesn't mean enough to you, you will fall short from achieving your goal.

- YOU'VE GOT TO DREAM – If you want a better future you have to dream. Without dreams and visions people perish and wilt away. Visualisation has become a huge part of my life over the last five years. When I sat down in December 2014, the Ironman was a dream. If I hadn't had that idea, then I wouldn't have developed the mindset required to achieve such a challenge. Dreams also need action, so once you're settled on your dreams and aspirations, it's important to organise a plan of action as to how to achieve it. Dreams are a key ingredient for anyone wanting to develop an iron mindset.

- NEVER GIVE UP – This is where it's really at, but it's easier said than done. No matter how low you get, if you commit to the plan and follow the advice in this book, then it will become easier to never give up. Personally, giving up is not an option. I've far too many motivations to keep achieving the goals I've set myself. Structure and plans keep you on point with this, but I'm telling you now, if you want to be a champion, then you can never give up. There have been many times at different periods in my life when I've asked myself 'Why bother? What are you doing this for?' It's at times like these that you know you have an iron mindset when you continue with your plan despite feeling mentally weak.

- RELY ON YOURSELF – It's incredibly important to be self-reliant. This means that you look to yourself to achieve whatever goals you've set. Nobody else is responsible for your success in life or your achievements, only you. How powerful is that? Take some time out and reflect on it: the goals you set yourself will only be achieved by your good self. If you want to do an Ironman, you have to become incredibly self-reliant and trust in your ability to carry through the tasks, the training, the nutrition goals you've set yourself. Do you trust yourself enough to achieve this? If you want to own your own business, do you trust yourself enough to put in the effort and commitment for it to be a success? My contact's list is full of people who have lofty ideas or notions that they want to do one thing or another or achieve something or complete a challenge. It all starts off very well, exciting, but after a month or two they fall off the wagon presenting some half baked excuse. You must be able to control your mind, your thoughts and trust yourself if you want to achieve that iron mindset that will allow you to hit your goals and achieve your dreams.

- LEARN FROM OTHER PEOPLE – It's important to become a good observer and a selective listener. What I mean by that is it's imperative you listen to people you admire and who have walked the talk, not people who are talking out their backsides and haven't got the T-shirt. There are lots of people telling anyone who wants to listen how to become successful, how to make money and how to build a business, but a huge percentage of these people haven't done any of the above, so how are they qualified to tell you how to do it? If you want to develop an iron mindset, make sure you get round the winners and tease conversation out of them. Ask them questions and for advice on how to navigate the journey of life.

A big part of me starting to believe the Ironman dream was possible was seeking out people who had already completed the challenge. I phoned them, met with them and talked about the challenge for quite some time. This gave me a unique understanding of what was required to get over the line. As Will Smith says, don't reinvent the wheel; learn from others' experiences.

- START TO READ BOOKS - If you don't already do it, then it's time to start reading books. Up until I was twenty-eight years old I read very little, but in the last ten years, since I immersed myself in reading and growing, I've now read hundreds of books. This has increased my knowledge and helped me ascertain essential life skills. I now know it's essential to read if you want to develop that iron mindset. The very inspirational motivational speaker Les Brown suggests we read thirty pages of something every single day. I've been doing this for the last five years and my life continues to grow and prosper. Go read some books and watch the difference it makes to your life and those you spend time with. I never thought I would have a library at home but I do, and every time I look at the books I've read, I feel a lot better for it.

- SAY ENOUGH IS ENOUGH – So, where are you in your life today? Is your life full of excitement and adventure? Are you pushing yourself out of your comfort zone every day, every week, or are you playing life safe and taking it easy – in other words not growing? There are too many of us just living and growing old carefully, and this is no way to live. We all need goals and challenges in life because that leads to structure, discipline, achievement and adventure. Too many people out there are fed up with the rut they find themselves in and something needs to change. That something is their thoughts. You can change your thoughts, actions and approach right now, today, tonight or tomorrow morning – it's up to you, you're in control. No one has a divine right to a great life, and your life is not someone else's responsibility. Like everything worth fighting for you have to work hard for this. You have to say enough is enough and get on with it. Run that 10k or that marathon, visit that exotic country, go watch that world title fight in Madison Square Garden, set up that business you've always wanted to, say hello to that girl you've been admiring for years. Enough is enough. It's time to grab life by the balls and start living.

- THINK RICH – Finally, and fittingly if you really want to develop an iron mindset, you need to start thinking rich. One of the most important and influential books I've ever read is a book which has sold over fifteen million copies, *Think and Grow Rich* by Napoleon Hill.

In this book Hill talks about the seventeen principles of success. Having read it many times, I'm now convinced that if you follow the principles and bring them into your own life, you'll develop the iron mindset you're seeking. It's unavoidable. There are two types of people in life: optimists and pessimists. Here is a genuine question - which one are you? Are you aware that it's medically proven that optimists tend to live longer, are more successful and live more adventurous and rewarding lives. Pessimists tend to die younger and lead more miserable lives. We are all the result of our thoughts, so with that in mind it's time to think rich.

There's a quote in Proverbs that says, 'As you think, so you become'. How powerful is that? I'm now only interested in putting good thoughts and positive images into my brain. I rarely watch television, as it's full of negativity and toxic material, the same with mainstream media and their publications. Instead I prefer to listen to podcasts, read books and seek out people who have brought achievement into their lives. It makes so much sense.

Do not underestimate how important it is to stand guard at the door of your mind and decide what you put into the mental factory otherwise known as your brain. My thoughts, actions and mindset are what have got me through my multiple sclerosis. Once I looked into my illness and where I was at in 2007, I refused to accept that this thing was going to define or destroy me, so I went about trying to reverse the illness. What did I do? Well, I pretty much followed the principles above: I read books, met people with the same illness and had endless conversations with them. I studied MS thoroughly and got interested in the role exercise and food could play in my recovery along with medication. When I felt I had the right level of understanding about the illness, I put my plan together to fight back and regain control of my life. I remember very clearly, September 2008, struggling to walk through my local grocery store to shop for provisions. Walking was a challenge for me with MS taking over my body. But I didn't give up. I continued to believe and work on my plan. When I crossed the finish line in Majorca in 2015, this was a major turning point in an incredibly powerful way.

I knew there weren't too many people across the world living with MS who had achieved what I had just achieved. This thought and the result of that day put me on a new pathway, where I would start yet another new journey in my life. I was buzzing with confidence, knew that I could achieve almost anything I put my mind to, and along with the significant impact it made on myself, even more empowering was the effect it had on my family and other people who drew great strength from my achievement.

If you want to develop your iron mindset, you need to start to think like a champion – an Ironman triathlete. You don't have to be one, but you do have to get to that level of thought, desire and will to win. Think rich, think like a champion and watch your life improve.

It's so important not to let what happens in life's journey define you or dictate your path. It's very clear if you look hard enough that you can achieve whatever you want despite what you and others think is possible. The vast majority of people do not realise their full potential, which is ultimately very unfulfilling for them individually and for those closest to them. With my newly revitalised trajectory in life, I'm focused on continuing my personal journey of growth and adventure, and I accept that for me to keep progressing I have to follow the code I've set out in this book. I'm now in a situation that feels like there is no better way for me to live, and I very much look forward to what the future holds for me. I know one thing for sure: it won't be all plain sailing, but I'm also certain it will be full of excitement, adventure and hopefully prosperity and fulfillment.

Ironman was an incredible journey for me. It was very tough, all of it, but it was an extraordinary achievement on a personal level and it gave me a feeling that I'm sure you only get when you cross the finish line of the magic carpet. If you're considering such a challenge, sign up straightaway. You'll not regret it, and will look back on it as one of your greatest and most exciting achievements of your life.

Two years ago I couldn't swim, and only a few weeks ago I completed my fourth Ironman race in the last twelve months – an awesome feeling. Remember, you need a 'why' to achieve the goals you set yourself. There has to be a big enough reason for you committing to the hard work in the first place. If you can find your why, then start that business, run that 5k race, seek out that relationship, fix that problem. Once you find your 'why' follow the roadmap in this book and I'm certain you'll develop that iron mind which will get you where you want to go

I hope you've enjoyed reading this book. I'm incredibly proud to have, yet again, completed another book and shared my experiences with you. I genuinely hope it inspires you to make the positive changes in your life, whatever they may be, which will allow you to go on and realise your potential.

Positive Change

In 2009 I set up my website, www.conordevine.com. The goal was to inspire and educate people on the subject of multiple sclerosis, to allow them into my world so that they could see how I was getting on in the hope that this would encourage them to bring a positive change into their own lives. Three years after my website went live I received an email out of the blue from a lady called Sam from El Paso, Texas.

> *Thank you for sharing your personal journey, Conor.*
> *I can now say today is a new beginning for me liv-*
> *ing with MS. I am truly going to live positive change.*

'Positive change'- what an empowering email, and how humbling for me to continue to get feedback of this sort from all corners of the world.

You are what you think you are, and it's now time to start believing in yourself more. If you implement a lot of what I've set out in this book, I have no doubt you'll feel the benefits in your life.

My own health continues to improve. I went vegan in January 2016 which has been a wonderful experience, and I was strong enough to give up my medication in April 2016 after ten long years fighting MS and injecting medicine. The medication I now utilise every day to reverse my illness is food and exercise. In the last six months I've reviewed my life and how I was living to see if there were changes I could make that would be beneficial. In my opinion this is something we should all do every three months – it's no different to getting your car serviced every year only humans need to lift the bonnet more than once a year in my view.

I paid particular attention to my diet to see if I could improve my nutrition enough to allow me to feel better. Thankfully, with the changes I made in January, the riches are starting to bear fruit as my MS symptoms are at an all-time low and my energy levels are going through the roof. I continue to get stronger and despite the storms I'm walking through on a very personal level, I'm focused on the positives in life which is making me stronger.

In my first book, *Attitude Is Everything*, the message was very clear: despite what you may be facing in life, if you approach the fences with the right attitude, then you have every chance of coming out the other side a lot stronger. Ironman is no different. Get your attitude right and everything else will fall into place.

My future looks incredibly exciting. Earlier this year when I met with Rich Roll I listened intently to his talk in which there were aspects that rang so true with many of my own experiences in life. I got the chance to speak with Rich that evening in Co. Wicklow, Ireland, and I asked him to sign my copy of his terrific new book *The Plantpower Way*. As well as autographing it he wrote, *'Your time to inspire'.*

I'm now ready to help as many people as possible develop a mindset that will hopefully help them realise their true potential. I'm going to do this through my website, my food, my exercise programmes, the challenges I take on, how I speak and interact with people, my blog, and above all else, my character and lifetime values.

Ironmind: Against All Odds is the start of a new phase in my life. A new phase in which I'll continue to grow and influence people in a positive manner. A way that will lead people to making positive changes in their own lives, beneficial changes for them, their families and their communities.

I wish you continued success in all your endeavours, and I ask one favour: if this book has affected you in a positive way, it would be great if you would let me know.

I'm not doing this alone; let's do this together. Let's build a happier, healthier world and help as many people as we can develop their own Ironmind.

Best wishes

CD

Printed in Great Britain
by Amazon